1001
RUNNING
TIPS

1001 RUNNING TIPS

THE ESSENTIAL RUNNERS' GUIDE

robbie britton

Vertebrate Publishing, Sheffield
www.v-publishing.co.uk

1001 RUNNING TIPS

THE ESSENTIAL RUNNERS' GUIDE

robbie britton

First published in 2021 by Vertebrate Publishing. Reprinted in 2022.

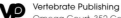 **Vertebrate Publishing**
Omega Court, 352 Cemetery Road, Sheffield S11 8FT, United Kingdom.
www.v-publishing.co.uk

Copyright © 2021 Robbie Britton and Vertebrate Publishing Ltd.

Robbie Britton has asserted his rights under the Copyright, Designs and Patents Act 1988 to be identified as author of this work.

A CIP catalogue record for this book is available from the British Library.

ISBN 978-1-83981-066-4 (Paperback)
ISBN 978-1-83981-067-1 (Ebook)

Front cover illustration © Julia Allum represented by www.meiklejohn.co.uk
All photography individually credited.

Design by Nathan Ryder, production by Jane Beagley and Cameron Bonser, Vertebrate Publishing.

Printed and bound in Europe by Latitude Press.

Vertebrate Publishing is committed to printing on paper from sustainable sources.

contents

introduction

Good advice doesn't have to be boring. Excellent, but boring advice isn't any use either, if no one reads it.

That's the maxim to keep in mind when jotting down the tips you are about to read (or are considering reading, if you're fortunate enough to be browsing in a wonderful bookshop).

In the hope of preventing this hefty tome from becoming a doorstop or, worse still, a pristine, unopened textbook on your shelf that one hopes to absorb via osmosis, I have jam-packed it full of solid advice and smiles.

If you read, and absorb, all 1,001 tips in this book, then you are guaranteed a new personal best (PB). This could be at any distance or event, but probably not the 800 metres.

A good book is dog-eared and worn. Favourites pages folded down; corners blunted from being carried around in a bag or passed to friends to borrow. My goal is for *1001 Running Tips* to become like this too.

The following pages contain a huge number of snippets of advice that come from my own experiences, both good and bad, as well as the experiences of friends, fellow athletes and coaches. Some of them you might already be familiar with, having learned from your own mistakes or having taken advice from mentors, but some will be new and hopefully will help you on your way. To some, 1,001 tips might sound like a lot, but when it comes to a subject that I'm so passionate about and have spent years and years dedicated to, the advice comes swiftly.

Over a decade ago I started out as an ultra-runner, who did a bit of coaching on the side. Now the tables have turned and I'm an endurance coach, who happens to indulge in a bit of running and cycling too. That doesn't mean I've lost my competitive edge, or have become resigned to a gradual decline in sporting performance as I move towards the grave, but I have found that the joy I get from helping others towards their own endurance goals is as great, or greater, than the pleasure I get from working towards my own goals.

Running is a simple sport. We choose to make it complicated, but when broken down into its fundamental parts it's just one foot in front of the other. Anyone can move from point A to point B. Be it five kilometres or 100 miles – if your life depended on it and time wasn't an issue, you'd get there.

What I hope these tips will do is make that journey a little bit easier. Good training prepares the body and mind for the challenges ahead; good fuelling makes the miles easier and the right kit can stop your nipples from being chafed into oblivion. So, whether you're just starting out or an experienced veteran of 100-mile racing, there is something in this book for you. I mean, with 1,001 tips, there must be something you've not heard before and, if not, I doff my cap. I've forgotten at least 200 of these since writing them.

As runners we are enamoured with progression. The real, tangible and often objective improvements that might be hard to find in other walks of life. A time or a PB can be oppressive if you can't beat it, but when you do beat it you know it's down to hard work. Or fancy new shoes.

I like to think the reason I was asked to write this book wasn't because of my outrageous running successes (there are plenty of faster, stronger or better runners than I am), and it probably wasn't down to my fantastic sense of humour (although it could be), but down to my willingness to risk failure, chase big dreams and learn from my mistakes.

A textbook might tell you how you are supposed to run, eat or train, but I want you to take the advice in these pages and go and experiment. Try, fail, reflect, learn and try again. Failure is seen as a bad word, but it's an opportunity to learn and hopefully this spirit is shared in the pages ahead.

Failures, lots of them, brought me to where I am today. Big dreams keep me working hard and doing my best to be a good athlete and coach, but even if I do ultimately fail to achieve all of my big goals in life, having a book published was one of them, so that's a win. Having raced from 3,000 metres up to 261 kilometres in one single day, across deserts, over mountain passes and through cities, the failures have come thick and fast, but the successes have kept my head above water too. Hopefully this book is one of the victories; it certainly feels like one.

There are way more than 1,001 ways to improve your running, but here are the best bits of advice I've been given, or learnt through blood, sweat and tears, in the world of running. Now go out for a run and read this book as a cool down.

acknowledgements

Firstly, I'd like to thank some of the brilliant people who have helped me throughout my life: my mum Sharon, my Nana, my wild Auntie Pauline, my wonderful wife Natalie, my Old Man (whose own history of running grew as my career did) and many more who have kept me on the not-so-straight and narrow over the years.

The ultra-running community has always been a special group of people, and I'll be forever grateful to be a part of it.

Thanks to my coach and friend, Tom Craggs. The man seems to know everything. Sophie Grant and Sarah Tunstall were also very generous with their time in answering questions for this tome.

Thanks also to Kirsty Reade, who for years has helped find a suitable place for my style of writing and humour, and to all those at Vertebrate Publishing who gave me the chance to fulfil a lifelong ambition of putting words into an actual book.

Lastly, thanks to the people who took the lovely pictures, especially the ones that include me.

feedback and updates

If you have any feedback or questions regarding this book, or if something has once again shifted with the sands of time, let me know at *robert.britton@live.com*

Constructive criticism is always welcome too. Our knowledge is always evolving, both as individuals and within our sport as a whole, but hopefully most of these tips will hold their value for a few years.

My website is *www.robbiebritton.co.uk*

There are plenty of articles and extra advice out there, mainly on *www.fastrunning.com*

Social media is just *@ultrabritton*

Try to take your eyes off the path occasionally to look at the view; if you're lucky it will be as stunning as this one. Here, Laura Hill is descending towards Stob Bàn in the Mamores.
© Keri Wallace, Girls on Hills – *www.girlsonhills.com*

Beware the half-stepper *(tip 4)*, especially if they have a topknot.   © *Tim Lloyd*

001

BASICS (1-72)

'Think long term, then work backwards from there. If you want to run a marathon then find interim goals along the way that you can work towards — celebrate these goals and signpost your progress.'

Jon Drever not smiling and therefore running slowly around Usk Reservoir in Wales. © *John Coefield*

BASICS (1-72)

THE RULES (1-11)

1. Whatever pace you run and whatever surface you run on, if you want to call yourself a runner then that's all that matters. Unless you're just walking, then you're a walker and that's okay too.

2. Training always counts, even if it's not on Strava. Unless it should be a rest day.

3. Be bold, start cold. You might be a little chilly going out of the door in shorts, but if you wear too much then you'll be dripping with sweat in no time and looking for somewhere to stash your jacket to collect on the way back.

4. Miles with a friend are always easier miles, no matter how hard you're working. It's scientifically correct as well, as our own perception of effort is changed when we run with someone else. Be wary if your training partner is a 'half-stepper' and always insists on running half a step in front of you, whatever your pace is.

5. The best kit is the kit that you already own. No amount of compression socks, carbon-plated shoes or designer caps will take the place of good, consistent hard work.

6. 'Racing is life. Everything before or after is just waiting.' Steve McQueen said this about motorcycles; it goes against my own ideas around finding fulfilment from your own training and adventures, but it sounds cool. However, if you like racing that much, you're getting something right.

7. Go to your local parkrun, whatever pace you run or walk. It's full of great people and, although it's not a race, you can race. That makes sense, right?

8. Join a club – they are the bedrock of endurance running. You'll find people to share miles with, learn from, race with and against; you'll also gain support and feel part of a community.

9. Smile – you'll run faster. It works for Eliud Kipchoge, but it may not be the only factor in his rather impressive marathon career.

10. Longer isn't always better. You might get more kudos for finishing a 100-miler, but reaching your true potential over a shorter distance can be just as satisfying.

11. Running is fun. If it stops being fun for more than one hill session, then step back and think about why. If you're not enjoying the training, the racing or even the community, then maybe you need to nap more.

STARTING OUT (12-36)

12. Depending on your level of fitness when you begin, the 'couch to 5K' programmes available online can be a good place to start. Starting out with a run and walk strategy will allow you to progress over time and then your body might be ready for more advanced plans.

13. When starting out, it's more about consistently going out for a run than attempting any fancy sessions, plans or gimmicks. Start by trying to get your running up to 30 minutes without stopping.

14. If you can already run for 20 or 30 minutes without stopping then the next step is consistency. Doing this three or four times per week, without negative impact or injury, should be the next simple goal. You could also try to extend the time of a single run per week to up to one hour.

15. At this point there are plenty of usable training plans, from multiple online sources (including *Runner's World*) or even in more advanced training books, that you can follow; just remember that none are made specifically for you.

16. Even if you do have a 'personalised training plan' that someone has made for you, your training and needs are very dynamic. What might be right for you one day can be a bad idea the week after, and you could even be progressing faster than the plan has allowed for.

17. View any training plan with a critical eye and don't be afraid to change and adapt it. Tired? Then move that interval session. Feeling good and want to add an extra rep in? Then think about its value and the impact it might have on the following days, but don't be afraid to experiment.

18. Be wary of how much you increase training at this early stage. The majority of issues for beginners (and experienced runners) come from doing too much too soon. Build up gradually; allow your muscles and tendons to grow stronger and more accustomed to what you're asking from them.

19. If you do experience an injury early on, then don't be dismayed. Really, it's 'welcome to the club', as the vast majority of runners experience injury each year. This doesn't mean we just accept it as a given, but you're not alone. Don't give up yet. (See **Injury** *(tips 475–506)*.)

20. The vast majority of your training should be what is referred to as 'easy running'. It's at the lower end of your aerobic ability, but is actually really important for your progression. You're building up your cardiovascular system, muscle capacity and endurance.

21. The biggest mistake a lot of runners make is overcooking the easy running. Professor Stephen Seiler's research suggests that this is the greatest difference between recreational and sub-elite runners. Easy running should be the bulk of your training. To safely manage more volume and to keep consistent you must make sure that your easy runs and days are actually easy.

22. Each run should have a purpose, but these aren't written in stone like the Ten Commandments. There might be a physiological reason for each session, but psychological factors matter too and sometimes a run can just be for letting off steam or having some fun. As long as you have a purpose for it, it can be of value to you, but remember that purpose as you're going along. If it is a recovery run, then keep that in mind so you ensure you're getting what you need that day.

23. There are several fancy ways to measure your effort level, from heart rate (HR) to blood lactate measurements, but the most effective tool for any runner is their own perception, otherwise referred to as 'rate of perceived exertion'.

24. Any magical watch or HR monitor can start registering that your heart is going to explode when you're simply jogging down to the shops, so it's important to learn how to gauge your own effort. Technology can be handy for measuring, analysing and interpreting your running, but it shouldn't dictate what you do.

25. An often-quoted golden rule for a runner wanting to progress is 'don't add more than 10 per cent additional volume each week', but remember we're all different. If you're only running for 30 minutes in total each week, then 40 minutes the week after is a 33 per cent increase, but you could just be changing two 15-minute runs into two 20-minute runs. This is a sensible progression, despite breaking the 'golden rule'.

26. When it comes to intensity and volume, try to increase one at a time. If you're building up your volume, then keep it simple and don't add additional faster running in too often as well. In simple terms, trying to run faster and longer at the same time can overstress the body.

27. Don't get carried away with progression either. We all get attached to the feeling of improvement, it's one of the joys of running regularly, but having down time and rest days, even recovery weeks, is the time you grow stronger and needs your focus too.

28. When starting out, it might be worth working with a two- or three-week cycle of progression, recovery and consolidation. We all think it's the hard sessions and increased mileage that brings home the bacon (or vegan alternative), but they're nothing without the sleep, recovery and easy running to allow the adaptations to sink in.

29. Now we're getting rolling, it's worth nipping the love of 'mileage' in the bud too. It's much more effective to think of training in terms of time than distance. Firstly, not all miles are created equal, with hills, mud, cobbles, headwinds and rain not only changing how long it takes to run different miles, but also the same mile on a different day.

30. Even running your normal loop in the dark is going to change how long each mile takes, and potentially change the impact that run has on your training.

31. Thinking in terms of distance is one dimensional, especially when we consider it takes many of us a different amount of time to run the same distance. If a beginner takes 30 minutes to run 5K and an experienced runner takes 15 minutes, should they be treating a 5K run in the same way? No, as it's twice as much training for the less experienced runner to go the same distance. If you think of your weekly training solely in terms of distance you can end up doing more training than is sensible for your level. Think of it in terms of time, still progressing as you improve, then you might make bigger leaps as you get faster, but it'll also take into account a whole host of other factors too.

32. Think not only of the time you are running, but also the time between those runs as well. Recovery time is important, especially if you start to run with more intensity. If you run one evening and then in the morning the next day, expect to feel the run from the night before and change your run accordingly. Holding off until the evening will provide 24 hours of recovery instead of 12, for example.

33. In the early stages, make sure you're enjoying yourself. The rush of endorphins comes quick and easy early doors – that glowing feeling of accomplishment for the first continuous run, a new PB on your home loop or feeling fitter and stronger, but a good, old-fashioned measure of whether you're pushing too much, too early is a big smile. If you're dreading the runs, grimacing your way through them and crying into a cup of tea afterwards, maybe ease back a little. Running should be fun, at least most of the time.

34. It's not just smiling, listen to your body as a whole. I keep harping on about individuality and there are plenty of common mistakes, but you know your body best and if something hurts, then maybe ease back a little. If you need to, get a professional opinion from a physiotherapist or go for a sports massage. Be wary of Dr Google. They'll suggest your legs are going to fall off.

35. It's worth taking a sensible progression through the distances and starting with some shorter races. There's no shame in focusing on 5K to get your PB down before stepping up to 10K. Just because Dave from the office is running 100 miles doesn't mean you have to go straight up to the marathon to catch up.

36. Progress sensibly with your race distances and you will be around in this sport for a whole while longer. Eliud Kipchoge has made a whole career going from 5,000-metre world champion in 2003 to marathon maestro and world record holder in 2018. He might never step up to 100-mile races, but we can only hope.

WHERE TO RUN? (37–41)

37. Head out of the front door, choose left or right and, if you don't know the area, use the tried and tested out-and-back. It's a fact of quantum physics that, no matter how fast you run the outward leg, you always get home quicker.

38. Before this new-fangled internet we used to use a map and compass to find our way around; maps were also great for planning running routes. Ordnance Survey allow you to order a map centred on your home location, so if you want to explore, that's a great way to start.

39. If in doubt, then there is often a local parkrun (their website always lists the route they take). If you're not yet up for going along on a Saturday morning, you could just try the route out on your own.

40. If you don't feel safe exploring on your own then local clubs will often have a wide range of groups, some for beginners and others for more experienced athletes, and they will take you on magical mystery tours of the local neighbourhood. When I started running with North Norfolk Beach Runners there was this great chap called Malcolm Ball who would lead us around the Cromer roads and trails, knowing every little hill to test us and always with a smile on his face. Malcolm has sadly passed away now, but every club has wonderful people just like him, helping a whole host of runners to discover their local area. Thanks Malcolm.

41. There are some great route-finding apps, my favourite being Komoot. You simply add start and finish points and the app finds you a route that can then be plugged into your watch (or your memory if you're bold). Using Komoot has often shown me little trails and shortcuts that I'd never have found on my own.

GOAL SETTING AND RACE CHOICE (42–56)

42. One of the great ways to keep momentum with early excitement is to pick a race goal. It doesn't need to be big and scary, but just popping something in the calendar, maybe even getting a couple of friends to sign up too, can maintain your focus after you begin running. I started by signing up for the Windermere Marathon with my friend Smithy. It was basically to prove I could, but also to stop Smithy having sole bragging rights about doing a marathon, as we'd have never heard the end of it. Whatever the reason, it got me out training, so find your reason to train.

43. Think long term, then work backwards from there. If you want to run a marathon then find interim goals along the way that you can work towards – celebrate these goals and signpost your progress.

44. Don't worry if some think your goals are unachievable. As long as you're willing to put in the time and effort to find out, then think big and believe in yourself.

A happy hound and a happy runner on the Lavaredo Ultra Trail, Italy. © Pete Aylward, RunPhoto

45. Talk to people you trust and respect in your sport. It could be a more experienced runner, a coach or just a friend who knows you well. Wanting to make the Olympic marathon team when you're still trying to break 30 minutes for the 5K might be a goal so far away that you'll be better off focusing on some targets a little closer to home first.

46. Running is a journey of discovery and if you're happy putting all your time and effort into finding out that something is truly unachievable, then there is value in that too. If, say, you want to be a 24-hour running world champion, but if you give it everything and come up short, then you'll be happy. It's not giving it your all that leaves you with regret.

47. Write your goals down. In a diary, on a piece of paper on the fridge or, as so many do these days, on social media. It's not about boasting to others about what you're going to do (action is more important than words in that regard), it's about accountability.

48. Tell your friends and family your goals. Stating that 'I'm going to run the London Marathon' might seem like a big challenge, but without your family on board it will be harder and just them knowing means you're less likely to skip that long run for a Netflix marathon instead (definitely not the same type of marathon).

49. Be SMART with your goals. It's a simple adage, but effective. It stands for Specific, Measurable, Achievable, Relevant and Time-based.

50. *Specific goals* are ones that are definable and clear so that you know what you are working towards and can focus your efforts on what is important to achieve your goal. 'I want to run faster' is different to 'I want to run fast enough to qualify for the Boston Marathon in 2025'.

51. *Measurable goals* allow you to see progress and actually know when you have achieved your goal. If your goal is simply 'I want to run better' then how do you measure this? 'Faster', 'more evenly paced' or 'with greater consistency' can all be measured, but simply 'better' cannot.

52. *Achievable goals* are important for motivation. As *tip 45* says, if it's so far out of reach that you can never get there, or at least you're struggling to visualise getting there, then something closer to home is needed. It might just be a step on the journey to that further goal, but it needs to be within reach.

53. *Relevant goals* mean that you're picking something that is important to you and where you want to be in the long term. Just selecting something achievable that your heart isn't set on, so that you reach your goals, will affect motivation, and not necessarily have the intrinsic value you need for long-term incentive.

Tracy Purnell and Jon Barton (who is displaying a perfect example of aeroplane arms – see *tip 302*) drop off Twmpa in Wales. © *John Coefield*

54. *Time-based goals* give you a schedule and a deadline to achieve your goal. Without a deadline there's every chance that you won't do what is necessary to get where you want to be, and with that the dream slips away. Tomorrow is great, but today is when you need to do the work.

55. Rope others into setting SMART goals too. Sit down (or just WhatsApp) with fellow runners and hold each other to account. You don't even need to have the same goals or events (or even set goals for the same sport or hobby), but just check in on each other to see how progress is going every week or two. It's amazing just how much checking in on each other will help.

56. Now sit down and think about what you need to do to achieve your goal. **Training** *(tips 73–84)*, **Strength and conditioning** *(tips 257–287)*, **Nutrition** *(tips 403–425)*, **Clothing** *(tips 720–757)* and **Staying motivated** *(tips 198–214)* might all play a part, some bigger than others, but make sure that you have a plan.

FELL, TRAIL AND MOUNTAIN RUNNING (57–72)

57. Off road running has plenty of names and it can get a little confusing, so here's a few descriptions to start and hopefully you'll have an idea of what you're potentially signing up for.

58. Trail running generally follows an actual trail that has been purpose built for hiking, running or biking. These vary from country to country and it's always worth finding out what constitutes a trail where you're heading.

59. How to spot a trail runner? They'll usually have a running vest and a fancy cap, sometimes worn backwards, and funky shades. Expect bright colours too, and calf socks.

60. Fell running is more likely to be on an open hillside. It originated as racing from a pub to the top of a local hill and back again. The races often don't have a set route and it is up to the athlete to decide on the best path between controls or checkpoints.

61. How to spot a fell runner? They'll be in a vest and shorts that were handed down to them by their mother or father, with shoes sporting at least one or two holes, and will shirk at paying more than £3.50 for a race entry, even with a free pie.

62. Hill running is what they call fell running in Scotland and Ireland. I think. How to spot a hill runner? They'll look like a fell runner, but with a Scottish or Irish accent.

63. Mountain running is the discipline practised by the World Mountain Running Association, who hold annual European and World Championships, which can be 'uphill only' or 'up and down' and usually take place on trails, but in mountainous environments.

64. How to spot a mountain runner? They'll often look pretty similar to a track or road runner, but with slightly more impressive calves. Look out for them training on mountain roads, rather than on the trails.

65. The International Sky Running Federation is a race organisation and business but has also come to represent skyrunning – the more extreme end of mountain running, on rockier and more technical trails and even off-trail, but still on set, flagged courses in the mountains. The races are all supposed to be above a certain height and have lots of ascent.

66. How to spot a skyrunner? Their knees will have a few scrapes from falling down on a pile of rocks; they might have some carbon hiking poles and a tiny waist belt that holds a thin jacket for the summit.

67. Orienteering is a combination of running and navigation, often in woodlands and off-trail, but also in urban environments, where the navigation plays a bigger part than in fell running, for example. It's popular in Scandinavia, but the UK and Ireland have some pretty good orienteers too.

68. How to spot an orienteer? A true orienteer will have a thumb compass on at all times and at the start of any run will look in all directions and could head off anywhere.

69. Snowshoeing is another discipline again, but as they have their own world championships, I guess they can have a tip or two. Using specially made, tennis racket-like contraptions to achieve a greater surface area, the athletes will race on top of a layer of snow.

70. How to spot a snowshoer? They'll have snowshoes on.

71. If you want to run in snowshoes then get some made for this purpose. The big, hiking ones will prevent you from actually running, but brands like TSL make some good lightweight ones and they can open up some wilder adventures for those who aren't a fan of skiing in the winter in mountainous areas.

72. Whichever type of running you find yourself doing, and all are great fun in their own right, it's okay to mix it up too. You might be able to work on strengths and weaknesses in a different format and take something back to your own discipline. Or you might jump ship to another side altogether.

Race packs can be really useful, even if you just wear them for a photoshoot with nothing in them. © *Tim Lloyd*

Team yellow at The Grizzly in Devon. © Pete Aylward, RunPhoto

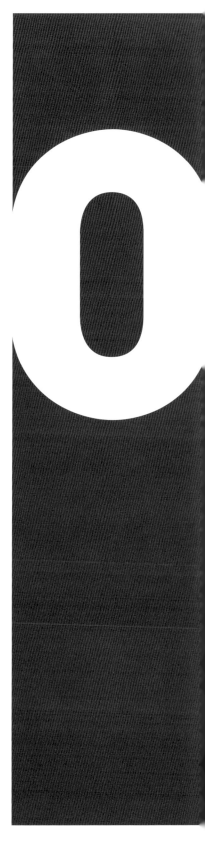

002

TRAINING (73–287)

'No plan survives a first contact with life.'

TRAINING (73-287)

BASICS (73–84)

73. A clear disclaimer to start the section: this isn't a training manual. Plenty of those exist and they're ace. These are the ramblings of man who's read a few of those (and used others as doorstops), undertaken coaching courses, gained some postgraduate qualifications, done a fair bit of coaching and worked with a whole host of people who know a lot more than me (such as Tom Craggs).

74. It doesn't mean that this section is full of garbage, but it's not the whole picture and doesn't go into nearly enough detail to make it comprehensive. This is the kind of book you read a few tips from while on the loo; it's not a complete training guide for coaches.

75. The way training works, on a very simple level, is that we stress the body, it recovers and grows stronger because of this process. Train, recover, adapt.

76. At first just get out running: experiment with different paces, effort levels and distances. It's important to build an understanding of your own body and running before a coach, watch or app starts telling you what to do.

77. Don't be afraid to get things wrong. Going too hard on the first kilometre or interval is a right of passage. If you interrupt your consistency because you need a week off with DOMS (delayed onset muscle soreness) then it's not a waste, as long as you learn a valuable lesson. Don't aim for DOMS, just learn from it if you get it.

78. It's not just a case of doing something really hard and then taking a week off and being better. Endurance athletes need to progressively overload their system over larger blocks of time, working on different stimuli, and recover, while maintaining the consistency of their training.

79. Good training is a balance between stress, recovery, consistency, progression, specificity and the big old jigsaw called life.

80. There are a whole host of different training sessions and focal points, but thankfully the world of running has got all the respective names and labels nailed down … well, things can get a little confusing.

81. You'll have heard loads of fancy terms such as VO_2 max, threshold running, steady running, tempo running, critical velocity, latte turn-point (the time of day after which it's inappropriate to have a latte in an Italian coffee bar) and a whole host more. *Tips 143–162* deal with different types of sessions but, for now, just remember that there needs to be variety.

82. A session can't just directly target VO_2 max, lactate threshold or cardiovascular systems, as much as it might read like this in some training manuals. It's not like we can turn off one aspect of our physiology and simply say 'sorry, I'm only working on my VO_2 max today'.

83. Think about how many running paces you actually need. If you're just starting out, then easy/medium/hard could be a good enough range to start with. Try running in a way that these three don't just melt into one pace or effort level, and that's a good start.

84. If you're already finding this section overwhelming, then you could consider hiring a coach or downloading a training plan. It doesn't mean you never have to learn about all this stuff, but a good coach will educate you along the way and can worry about a lot of this mumbo-jumbo for you, sometimes forever. Even a stock training plan hopefully takes the basics into account; then you can use *tips 85–109* to make it work for you.

TRAINING PLANS AND DO YOU NEED
A COACH? (85–109)

85. You don't *need* a coach. Plenty of people are capable of finding their own way in the world of running, but there are pros and cons to having someone help out.

86. Yes, just having the title 'coach' doesn't really mean anything and really you want to be looking for a good coach, not just someone who's given themselves the title to earn some cash. How does one find out if someone is a good coach or not? Ask around, speak to their athletes, their ex-athletes, the coach themselves and if they're holding a group session then why not ask to come along?

87. Don't just go based on their results. Research within my own Master's degree suggested that the longevity of coach–athlete relationships was a better measure of coaching success than results alone. Simply put, a bad coach could give an extremely hard and damaging training plan to 20 athletes, with little or no extra input, and one of those athletes might survive to run some good races before returning to the injury table. Is that good coaching and is it what you're looking for?

88. A coach isn't just a training plan, it's a whole lot more. A good coach will guide you through many aspects of your running career and some have different specialisms, such as race nutrition or sports psychology, but ultimately a good generalist, with interests in all areas of running, can help you avoid some of the pitfalls they have probably fallen into themselves.

89. A key element in any successful coach–athlete relationship is trust. An athlete must trust that their coach has their best interests at heart, trust in the coach's training and trust them enough to be open and honest. A coach must be able to trust that an athlete is being transparent and truthful with them. It's certainly a two-way street.

90. Self-coached athletes still see success and there are plenty of examples of this. A coach doesn't even need to be writing your training plan, they could simply be a sounding board for you to bounce your own ideas and training plans off. This might be more along the lines of mentorship; building a strong support network to discuss your training and racing with is always going to be useful, whether you're self-coached or not.

91. All the training books in the world, even this one, can't replace experience, self-reflection and a good network of peers. You don't need to do all this alone, so ask yourself, 'could a coach add something to my running?' It's not just handing over responsibility for everything, it's a partnership to improve your running.

92. A bad coach can certainly do more damage than good to your running career and often the impact goes on much longer than the actual coach–athlete relationship. Don't underestimate the impact fellow runners, coaches and peers can have on how you think of and view your running.

93. Don't just listen to a coach's advice on this though – I've clearly got a vested interest! Speak to other runners. Be wary of simply posting on social media as it seems each coach has an army of tweeters advertising their services.

94. If you are self-coached then self-reflection is even more important. Keep a training log, write about how you feel, how the day was and how the session felt. Having the opportunity to look back and see how that last taper or marathon session went when compared with previous sessions is invaluable.

Local runner John Price making it look easy on the Blorenge in Wales. © *John Coefield*

TRAINING (73-287)

95. Talk to other runners or coaches if you can. Just because you're self-coached doesn't mean you have to do everything on your own, especially if it's a new race or distance you're training for.

96. If you do take a stock training plan off the internet or from a book then don't be afraid to adapt it for you and your goals. We're all different and no stock plan is right for everyone. Some simply are not right for anyone …

97. Try to understand how and why the training plan is set out the way it is. Why does the 'long run' in the plan become steadily longer, but the next week it's shorter again? How do the intervals push me and why is the recovery between each smaller this week? Understanding a plan means you can adapt it; if you know the purpose of a session you can ensure that you're getting what you need from it.

98. It's not simply a case of doing a particular number of sessions in a week. It's like a recipe; the order in which you do things matters, it's not just bunging all the ingredients into a pot and hoping for the best.

99. Your own training is a constant journey, and very dynamic. What worked one week, or for one training cycle, might not be right for you the next time. Train, adapt and grow, then your body will need a different stimulus to keep improving, but maybe only slightly different.

100. Remember it's not just the hard sessions that count. Too often I see athletes squeezing their intervals or hills into the end of the week, as they think that's a better option than missing them out if they've got behind with their training. Your consistency is the top factor, so playing catch up with interval sessions at the weekend can lead to injury and tiredness. It's better to look at why you're playing catch up in the first place.

101. If you're short of time, a 30-minute easy run to keep the ball rolling is often better than just skipping your session, even if you'd planned a more structured and longer workout.

102. No plan survives a first contact with life.

103. In general, avoid higher-stress sessions, such as intervals, hills or long runs, on back-to-back days. Your body needs to recover to grow stronger, so hitting it with continuous hill workouts *(tip 157)* won't be the best thing for you.

104. As to any 'rules', there are exceptions and different ways of doing things. Follow Renato Canova's 'special blocks', do the odd back-to-back long run or simply do an easy, long run the day after a hill session. This can have a place in your training, but consider the impact and be wary of stressing the body in such a big way too often.

105. Don't just follow someone else's training plan. The number of people who have tried to copy sessions from runners such as Steve Way, Kilian Jornet or Aly Dixon and come unstuck is astounding. Take lessons from them, adapt to your own level and experience, but be smart.

106. One example is copying distance. Steve Way, with his 2:15 marathon PB, runs 100 miles a week in 10 to 12 hours, but if Bob, 4:28 marathon PB, copies his training plan and it takes him 20 to 24 hours to run 100 miles, then he's not doing the same training as Steve, he's unintentionally doing twice as much training as an international marathon runner. Steve Way's training blogs are a thing to behold; if you've not checked them out then go have a look-see, but don't copy them exactly. Look at the whole story of a late-starting athlete who progressed over the years to a very high level, but not without his share of troubles and injury too.

107. Consider a coach's motivations. No one enters coaching because they're an evil genius, but if your own business or employment is tied directly to results then it might be tempting to make decisions that aren't necessarily fully centred on the athlete.

108. All coaches want their athletes to do well – it makes us look good – but athlete health and long-term development also need to be important factors in training and can sometimes be secondary focuses.

109. Whether you're coached, self-coached, or somewhere in between, it can be very individual, so find out what works for you. If you are working with a coach then building a lasting relationship over time will help you get the most out of coaching too.

EFFORT LEVELS (110-142)

110. There are many different types of effort levels or running sessions to use, each with a different focus and desired stimuli. Some of them are exactly the same but with different names.

111. Variety, by continuing to stress the body in different ways with different sessions, can be a key to progression. Learn about different ways to challenge yourself and think about the purpose of any session you do.

112. Your sessions don't need to be complicated; understanding different training zones in great detail isn't a prerequisite for your running. Even having a simple breakdown such as easy/medium/hard will help you progress and keep variety in your training. As long as you can actually tell those effort levels apart. Just easy and hard is better than nothing.

113. The next level could be considering factors such as lactate threshold *(tips 124–131)* and your race paces. It really depends on the demands of the race and your current level.

114. Getting into heart rate, power and rate of perceived exertion could be some of the next directions you head in. Some runners use four or five different heart rate zones, but really, if you want to make things right for you, then it's worth getting a physiological test done in a sports lab to work out your zones.

115. While we're on heart rate, the gold standard piece of kit is a chest strap HR monitor *(tips 794–798)*.

116. The humble easy run is a good place to start when you want to assess your effort levels. Easy running is one of the areas that most runners could improve in, but not by going faster. Most runners do their easy running too hard, thus limiting how much of it they can actually do and affecting their faster sessions negatively through tiredness and fatigue.

117. Easy running will help increase capillarisation and blood volume, which means that more oxygen gets to the muscles and the muscles can use the oxygen more efficiently too. Don't write off easy running as being without value.

118. How easy should easy be? It's better to think of it as a range that covers anywhere from walking to, for some, up to 80 per cent of your maximum heart rate. It will vary based on how experienced you are, where you are in your current training progression and what you want to get out of the session.

Steep, rocky terrain, as tackled here by Sarah Macdonald in Glen Coe, is a great way to challenge yourself as a runner. © *Keri Wallace, Girls on Hills* – *www.girlsonhills.com*

The next generation totally smashing it at the Saturday morning parkrun.
© Pete Aylward, RunPhoto

119. The day after a hard interval session or race I might rest or maybe go for a recovery run. This, for me, is the easiest of easy runs, so it is very low intensity, and the main purpose is simply to get the blood flowing around the muscles without doing any additional damage. It might speed up as the run goes along and the body warms up, but the entire run is going to be pretty easy.

120. Go back to *tip 21* and Professor Stephen Seiler's research. The bulk of your training should be easy, especially when you are trying to increase your overall volume of training. It lowers the stress on the body but allows for a greater amount of adaptation through training.

121. Try not to worry about pace on your easy runs, unless you're targeting shorter distances, such as 5K to a half marathon. In this case you don't want the bulk of your running to be too far from your race pace, so a fair amount of your easy running might be at the higher end of what one would consider easy.

122. For marathon training, your pace depends on your experience, but some suggest that you should be keeping the bulk of your easy running closer to your marathon pace plus a minute (per mile), whereas others don't focus on pace quite as much.

123. For ultra-running, your race pace is going to be closer to your easy pace than likely any other pace you run in training, particularly if you're looking at 100-milers and 24-hour races. This means that you're getting the specific benefits of 'race pace' when you shuffle round the block first thing in the morning, plus some improvement of your ability to utilise fat as fuel *(tips 170–172)*.

124. When you're getting to the serious end of things you might hear people talking about lactate threshold. This is something that can be measured in the blood as your effort level increases. It's actually a type of fuel for the muscles, but it is accepted that it rises in line with hydrogen ions and blood acidosis, which will stop you in your tracks.

125. We have lactate threshold and lactate turnpoint. The first, lactate threshold, is the point where there is too much blood lactate for our bodies to process and dispose of while we continue running, so blood lactate (and its associated bad friends) start to accumulate. You can normally run for about an hour at this intensity.

126. Lactate turnpoint is where things get a little more serious and the rate we're accumulating blood lactate is way beyond what our bodies can utilise and dispose of. Basically, beyond this point, trouble is fast approaching.

127. Think of it as a rowing boat in the sea with a leak. When we row we can quite easily get rid of enough of the water coming on board before it becomes a problem. Work a bit harder, so your boat goes faster, and more water comes onboard; eventually over time it'll fill up and sink. Going above lactate turnpoint means waves are crashing over the side and you're filling up fast.

128. For many, the end of easy running is that first lactate threshold, where it starts to become unsustainable over a long period of time. It's not simply one exact point, but a range that will change and adapt over time.

129. Quite simply, we can improve our body's ability to sit in this zone by training in and around it. Let the body become more efficient at processing blood lactate and its associates, then you can stay in this zone for longer.

130. For those starting out, this will be your steady running. It's not easy, but it's not really hard, at least at first. Twenty minutes of threshold running will certainly feel tough.

131. I have often explained this to runners as going along at a steady effort, but with a couple of extra gears not being used. If your coach, or a lion, were to jump out of a bush and make you go faster, then you'd be able to up it a notch or two. If you're working harder than this for your threshold runs, then that's a little too much.

132. Then we move on to harder efforts than in your lactate workouts, at race paces that you can only sustain for 20 minutes or less. Normally one might use 5K, 3K or 1,500-metre race pace as terminology here, but it depends on what your times are for these distances, whereas thinking in terms of time allows us to understand more easily.

133. The best training plans will include a variety of paces to train around, ultimately built around your final race goals. If you're training for a 5K then this might range from a 400-metre race pace all the way through to a half marathon effort, whereas a marathoner might work from a 3,000-metre race pace upwards. Bear in mind that touching base with your faster paces, even as a marathoner or ultra-runner, will certainly help.

134. Keeping the leg speed ticking over with 'strides' can also be an option. These are simply bursts of acceleration and holding a strong pace for a short amount of time or distance. They can be completed at the end of an easy run without much impact on the following day's training.

135. Strides shouldn't be aerobically hard work; you're looking to work on the muscle patterns, holding good form and recovering fully in between. They can be anything from 10 to 15 seconds, up to more controlled 20 or 30 stride-outs. You're stopping before it feels like hard work.

136. Strides can also be useful before a harder session or race, either in the warm-up or on the day before, to prepare on a neuromuscular level for the task ahead. It's much more specific than just doing a slow or progressive run that doesn't touch on the pace you will hit when the gun goes off.

137. All of the paces and effort levels listed above, plus the other terminology out there, such as critical velocity, VO$_2$ max work and maximal steady state, can be worked into a variety of sessions and training types.

138. What's next? Well, that depends on the distance you're focusing on, but not every interval needs to be all out. What's the smallest possible 'dose' of training that will get the improvement you need?

139. Think of your intervals as poison (bear with me) and you want to build up an immunity to this poison. What dose of poison can you stand on a day-to-day basis that won't kill you, but will build up the immunity? A minimum effective dose. There are other ways to build up your ability to cope with this poison – a healthy diet and adequate recovery, for example. Think of each easy run as a little dose of poison and intervals, long or tempo runs as a much bigger dose. Too much too soon, and you're dead (read: injured), but building up progressively over time, allowing time to recover and deal with larger and larger doses, and you will build up that tolerance for the big event, when your editor tries to poison you for using terrible analogies (or a marathon, where each mile at marathon pace is a dose of your favourite poison).

140. Don't actually micro-dose poison, only training. Just in case you were wondering. No one is trying to poison you, we're not in a Victorian crime novel.

141. It's not possible to just target one type of stimulus, such as VO$_2$ max or threshold running, as the body will adapt in multiple ways from one run. Thinking about all the ways your body will benefit, or be impacted, by a session will provide a greater understanding.

142. Is coaching a science or an art? It's probably bit of both, especially when it comes to creating different types of session. While one must consider the physiological focus, there's also the psychological stimuli and how each individual session fits into the bigger picture too. One can vary the time, intensity, length and recovery between intervals, the terrain can be an additional challenge and even adding mental or strength tasks into a run can change things too.

TYPES OF SESSION (143–162)

143. *Fartlek* is Swedish for speed-play and it's just that: playing around with different speeds, different intervals and normally the environment around you. It might be going hard from lamp post to lamp post, slowing down every time you pass a bench or even just totally unplanned interval lengths with friends, each taking turns to shout stop.

144. Progression running is the gradual build-up of speed as time progresses in a run. Start a progression run too fast and you will run out of speed to use before the end. Nine out of every ten progression runs, you will inevitably start too fast, and end up with nowhere to progress but the gates of hell for the last five or ten minutes. Avoid this if you can.

145. Interval running is often misunderstood as the hard bit being the interval, but it's actually the rest and recovery in between that is the interval. Basically, it allows the runner to maintain a faster pace or higher quality overall effort to their run, because there is time built in to allow some recovery.

146. Repetitions, or reps, are the faster parts of any interval session and these can also be constructed in sets. For example, in 4 × (4 × 400 metres), the reps are '400 metres', whereas the sets are '4 × 400 metres'. There is normally a shorter rest between reps and a longer rest between sets.

147. The size of the interval can instantly change the stimuli of the session. Take 10 × 400 metres, a simple enough session. If the rest is 30 seconds then it's more of a threshold workout, whereas if the rest is three or four minutes then you're working more on out and outright speed (although you'd likely reduce the number of reps if this were the case). The same goes for the rest between sets as well.

148. Tempo running is a term that is used in contrasting ways by different coaches and in different training philosophies, but describing it as 'holding a set tempo for the course of the run' allows us to cover most of the different usages. A 10K-pace tempo and a marathon-pace tempo are different effort levels, but the same type of session.

149. Threshold running *(tips 124–131)* is sometimes referred to as tempo running. A threshold workout could be run as a tempo run, in one go, or split into different blocks, such as efforts of 3 × 10 minutes.

150. The goal is still to have the body in and around the lactate threshold zone for extended periods of time, so even 20 reps of 400 metres with 30-second rests could be a threshold workout as the short rests don't allow the body to recover sufficiently to make the session about speed. This would potentially be a more suitable threshold session for someone focusing on higher-paced events such as 3,000 metres or 5K.

151. Sandwich sessions are another type of session that can mean different things to different groups. For an ultra-runner this is a session where you run at your race pace and try to eat a variety of sandwiches along the way. It prepares the gut but also helps you develop correct breathing patterns for when you mouth is full of cheese roll.

152. The more traditional sandwich session can have an athlete working on a variety of effort levels and can be very useful to many athletes. With a warm up and cool down on either side, there could be five or ten minutes of threshold or marathon-pace running either side of a shorter interval session. For example:
- 10 minutes marathon pace
- 2 minutes easy pace
- reps of 8 × 90 seconds at 5K pace (with 60 seconds recovery in between)
- 2 minutes easy pace
- 10 minutes marathon pace

TRAINING (73-287)

153. Any session that gets an athlete working on different paces and effort levels could be referred to as a multi-pace session. These can be useful for keeping an athlete in touch with faster paces as training builds and obtaining the desired stimulus in different ways.

154. Over-unders are an example of a multi-pace session that can be very useful. It could be 10 lots of three minutes at marathon pace with three minutes of steady running in between, or even just above and below the race pace you're targeting. For example, a marathoner could run for 16 kilometres and switch pace each kilometre, alternating between a pace of 10 seconds faster than marathon pace and 10 to 15 seconds slower than marathon pace. The end product is still 16 kilometres of running at your average marathon pace, but it can provide a greater effect than just running at a constant pace, although both sessions can have a place in a training cycle. A race isn't often run at a constant pace throughout, so this also helps us to cope with the demands of real racing.

155. If your session is very complicated, some watches can be programmed to tell you what to do, but the old-fashioned bit of paper or writing on your arm can help too. Be wary of losing your notes when you get sweaty though.

156. Hill sessions can be a type of session in their own right, working on the strength and speed of the runner by adding a gradient into the mix. They can also form a part of any of the above types of sessions too. For example, you can do an interval workout or threshold running on hills too. In some cases, if your race calls for this specific type of training, say it has a 40-minute hill climb in the middle, then you're best getting as specific as you can to align with the route of the race.

157. Continuous hills, or Kenyan hills, is another type of workout. This is basically a threshold workout with blocks of work done on either an undulating loop or a single 45- to 60-second hill climb. The important part is keeping your effort level, not necessarily pace, consistent for the up and the down sections of the run. It can be a great conditioning workout for those who have races with long downhills and none to practise on nearby, but also for strength for the latter stages of road marathons or cross-country racing.

158. For some there can be relevance to downhill efforts and drills, but the impact of these on your legs mean they've got to be worthwhile for you to consider them. Most fell runners will add them out of season during the winter and spring. See **Downhill running** *(tips 288–318)*.

159. If you find that you don't really enjoy one type of session in particular, then have a think about why this could be. Maybe that session is really focusing in on one of your weaknesses and you're going to get some real good bang for your buck. Or it might just be that you're pacing it like a wally.

160. The long run *(tips 163–175)* is one of my favourite workouts, closely followed by intervals, hill sessions and fartlek. Actually, it's just progression runs I don't really like that much (which is normally down to poor pacing).

161. Almost as important as the types of sessions themselves is the recovery time between them. This is most important with the idea of the weekly long run.

162. This is not an exhaustive list of types of session, especially if you start to consider all the different disciplines of running. If you enjoy a particular type that I've not mentioned, then please do share.

Jon Drever in his fell runner uniform in the Black Mountain, Wales. © *John Coefield*

TRAINING (73–287)

THE LONG RUN (163–175)

163. The traditional Sunday long run is in many training plans, but it doesn't always have to be on a Sunday. Working on a 10- to 14-day cycle can be better for some athletes as it allows greater space for recovery between sessions, but it might be difficult to fit in with work and family.

164. Long runs can be easy, steady or even pretty darn hard, but runners often find they have the biggest impact on their training and fatigue levels.

165. When planning a long run think of it in terms of time, not just mileage. It might be just the weather, but also terrain, elevation and training experience can all affect how long a 30-kilometre run takes for one individual on a particular day.

166. The old-school method of simply progressively increasing the length of your long run each week is a bit flawed. Firstly it doesn't allow for easier weeks, to enable the body to recover and adapt, but it also oversimplifies the long run as simply long slow distance and it can be so much more than that.

167. A simple long run might all be done at an easy pace, but it doesn't have to stop there. Adding in blocks of race pace, for half or full marathon, even ultra-distances, can be a very useful addition to a long run. An hour of easy running followed by three lots of 15 minutes of marathon-pace work (with five minutes of easy pace in between) can have a greater training stimulus, but also help a runner get used to how those legs will feel in the latter stages of a race and be good for practising race fuelling.

168. Race-paced long run effort can also be very costly in terms of training load too, especially if you're doing big blocks of half or full marathon pace. Breaking them up with easy intervals and not overcooking it can help you avoid leaving your best performance in a training run.

169. See every long run as an opportunity to practise race day fuelling, including dinner the night before, breakfast on the morning of your run and then actual run fuelling. This is obviously more valuable the more your run conditions match the conditions you'll face on race day, from pace and time of day, to temperatures and terrain.

170. Some runners like to do their long runs fasted with the idea being that it helps boost the body's ability to utilise fat as a fuel. I prefer faster to fasted, as running on empty will mean you have to slow down and potentially lower the benefit of that run, especially if you're targeting faster races like a half marathon or below.

171. Add to this the greater physiological cost of a fasted run, where the levels of muscle damage and fatigue can be greater, and it can interrupt the quality of training in the week to come. This goes for smashing those long runs too hard as well. Everything comes with a cost to the week after; finding balance is key.

172. Another reason against doing all your long runs fasted is that one of the biggest areas those racing marathons and longer can improve is fuelling *(tips 426–474)*. Every long run is a chance to practise your race fuelling; there is evidence that your gut can be trained to process higher amounts of carbohydrates while running too.

Make a plan, have a spreadsheet, bring a clipboard, but be prepared for it all to go out of the window at some point. © Robbie Britton

173. Test your kit out on those long runs too. Shoes that are fine for five one-hour runs a week might give you a blister after a two-hour run, or shorts that prevent chafing on an easy run might cause a problem when you hit kilometre 25.

174. Some will plan their long runs to coincide with training races. This can be useful if you struggle to go the distance on your own (although think about pacing and nutrition if this is the case) and it also adds a potential benchmark in your training timeline too.

175. Be aware that your training load will be high when you're doing training races, so don't get too dismayed if you don't smash that PB. Ideally, you're not going all out in these training races too; always keep something back with an eye on next week's training and your main goal race. A half marathon PB can be a nice addition along the way, but if it stops you getting that marathon PB because you needed a week off to recover then, all of a sudden, it's not that valuable.

ULTRA-LONG RUNS (176–183)

176. All the factors that are relevant for the long run become even more important if you're an ultra-runner. The longer you run for, the less your simple physiological fitness can be relied on. You need to have comfortable kit, good fuelling and hydration practices and be happy being out on the roads or trails for longer.

177. You don't need to run massive miles to train for an ultra. The same basic rules around getting physiologically fit still apply and variety of training is still important, but you need to work on progressing your ability to run for a long distance over time.

178. When you're training for an ultra-run it's important to look back over years, rather than months, as a lot of the lessons and value in an ultra-run don't fade over time like your fitness might. For example, if you're doing a 50K then your last marathon will have provided good lessons, moving up to the point where if you're running 200-mile races then the last 10 years of racing will have built your experience.

Serious game faces at the Goring 10K in Oxfordshire. © Pete Aylward, RunPhoto

179. In the specific 10- to 12-week block for training for your ultra you might have one or two purposefully long runs, but beyond a certain point, which varies based on experience, you're losing more than you gain. Even athletes I coach for the 24-hour IAU World Championships are maxing out at six hours and that'll only be once in the 10 to 12 weeks beforehand. They have years of long runs and races in the past which provide a lot of the logistical experience and I'm focused on making them physically fit and confident for their race without being exhausted or injured on race day.

180. Think about recovery from your long runs too. If you are new to ultras, then firstly don't jump up in distance too quickly. You need to learn from a 50K race, some 50-milers and maybe some 100K races before you step up to 100 miles. You can't learn everything you need in 10 to 12 weeks of training like you might for a marathon (and even then, it's better to work up to it over the years with some half marathons and 10-milers before).

181. If you want a bigger run in your build-up, then think about how long you'll need to recover from it and work backwards from race day. If you want to race a 50K in the build-up to your 100K, then give yourself the time to grow and adapt to that stress.

182. Add specificity to your long run too. If training for a mountainous or hilly race, you'll get more benefit from doing your long run on similar terrain and with similar environmental conditions.

183. If you can, do pre-race long runs on the course of the race itself. You can't get more specific, you'll familiarise yourself with the challenges you might face on race day and you might even be able to get some of your fellow racers to join you for a recce. Be aware of the race director's wishes on course recces though. Some events have special arrangements with landowners which only apply for race day. Some fell and trail races would be put in jeopardy if everyone ran the private sections of a course before race day and permission was removed.

THE CHAOS OF PERIODISATION (184-197)

184. Periodisation is the breakdown of training into more manageable chunks: yearly, monthly or weekly cycles that allow extra detail where needed, but also a vision of the overall work being done. Thinking about how you periodise your training will help you achieve your goals and peak at the right time to achieve them.

185. The traditional periodisation model is like a pyramid. You build your large foundation (base training) and then build smaller, but faster, blocks on top until you have the finished, super speedy article. It's more commonly used for half marathon distances and below, where outright speed is most important.

186. Another theory, especially for marathon distances and beyond, is almost a reverse periodisation. Start by working on the faster stuff, which is furthest away from what you'll do in a race, then get more specific to your goal the closer you get to the start line.

187. There are plenty of other ways to split up your macro- (maybe 16 to 20 weeks up to yearly), meso- (around four to six weeks) and micro- (weekly) cycles. How an athlete responds to training stimuli can be very individual. If someone tells you they've cracked the code for all runners, then be wary, very wary.

TRAINING (73-287)

188. Now watch your plan go horribly wrong in week four and slowly realise that all plans need to be adapted as you go along. Periodisation is a lovely theory that looks great in a textbook, but add in the variety of life and potentially watch chaos ensue.

189. Don't just throw the plan out of the window at this point though. Academic and coach John Kiely suggests that we've only really tested periodisation against non-varied, identical week-to-week training and that it might not be the way that training cycles are linked together which is important, but simply the fact that variation is involved.

190. Starting with a bigger, periodised plan is great, but you must be willing to adapt. Injury, illness, intermediate goals, family, life, work and a whole host of other factors will get in the way of our perfectly laid out plans and people simply react differently to what is prescribed for training.

191. Don't get too caught up on 'you have to do X before you do Y' in the structure of your training and keep in mind that most plans are built back from race day, not forward towards it.

192. There is no set amount of training, speed work, intervals, tempo running or marathon-pace running you have to do before a race. It's all very individual and relates to your own experience and context. I know people who've run 100-mile races well by training for 30 miles per week, yet elite 10,000-metre runners could be clocking up well over 120 miles per week. What's important is finding what is right for you.

193. Normally a training block for one race will be 10 to 12 weeks, possibly up to 16 weeks, because any more and it can be hard to stay motivated, fit and healthy for a singular goal. These 16 weeks, plus a four-week recovery period, might be your full macro-cycle for this section; but remember, it's not just racing that is hard on the body, the weeks of training will take their toll.

194. Growth from training comes in easier weeks; downtime to recover after tough blocks and races can be vital for longevity in the sport. Even swapping out for some **Cross-training** *(tips 246–256)* in between macro-cycles can be an effective way of avoiding burnout and injury.

195. Progressive loading of training, to keep up the stress that stimulates growth and improvement, needs easier weeks to sink in. Some runners use a 10- to 12-week block as almost one continuous stress on the body and only recover fully in their taper. Others will take an easier week every three to four weeks, so after each meso-cycle the body is given time to adapt to the overload and stress, starting the next meso-cycle fresh as a daisy … ish.

196. If you're finding yourself picking up injuries in these three- to four-week blocks, then don't be afraid to take an easy week every two, or even a few easy days after each 10 days. The structure of your weekly micro-cycle is going to include rest and recovery too, but tinkering with the bigger picture can help you stay injury-free and build that consistency.

197. This is also where a coach or a trusted friend can help. We all second guess if we are doing enough or too little, but having someone looking over your training to say 'you're progressing well' or 'don't worry, you're doing enough' can take a real weight off your shoulders.

STAYING MOTIVATED (198–214)

198. Even the most dedicated athletes can suffer from peaks and troughs in motivation and the first thing to remember is that it can happen to all of us, there's usually a reason behind it and it's okay to feel that way.

199. Motivation can wane for a number of reasons, but the first thing to look at is the overall load of your training and life. If you're knackered, from work, running, family or a combination of all these factors, then it can make getting out the door even harder.

200. Getting stuck in a rut can also be down to your training. If you're repeating the same sessions, in the same locations, without much progression, then it's hard to keep excited about your running. Even just mixing up where you do your easy running could have an impact.

201. Jumping in puddles is good for the soul. If you're feeling down, then find an extra muddy route and go and make yourself smile. Make sure to take your kicks off before going back in the house though.

202. Self-determination theory, developed by academics Edward Deci and Richard Ryan, can provide a great insight into an athlete's motivation. Having ownership over your goals and training, feeling that you are progressing and being socially connected to your sport can all boost motivation levels.

203. Some think that being coached means that you have no control, but you should make your coach–athlete relationship a partnership. If you don't feel like you can choose your own goals or have no control over your sessions, it can hamper progress.

204. Socialising in your running might seem like an added bonus, but it can be vital to progress. The long-distance runner may be seen as a lonely profession but, in reality, you're part of a tribe. If you go out on the Sunday long run or track Tuesday, then you're one of us. Feeling like you belong is important.

205. It doesn't even have to be how you train; what you wear can also bring some sense of belonging, like your first cycling cap making you feel a little bit more like Eddy Merckx. For runners it might be shorts, a singlet, jazzy tights or a go-faster 80s-style headband. Feeling like you belong really does help. Although don't be tricked into thinking total retail therapy is the answer. Look for kit you actually need that will last the test of time, rather than a cheap plastic bit of rubbish that you won't use after one or two runs.

206. Having realistic, timely and achievable goals will help with your motivation *(tips 42–56)* but also knowing you're progressing towards them too. If you're feeling low in motivation, then you could try looking back on older training diaries just to show yourself how far you've come.

207. The situation could feel a bit different if you've been out injured for a long time or have taken time off from running. In this case looking back, especially with those rose-tinted specs, can take some of the joy out of your current running. Yes, you used to be able to run four-minute miles for days on end in your youth (don't worry, no one can actually do this, they just didn't measure the courses correctly), but today, are you trying your best in the current situation? That's all we can really ask of ourselves.

TRAINING (73–287)

208. Comparison on social media can be unhealthy too, because firstly if you're following your running idols then it's setting a very high bar for comparison; but remember too, social media often only shows the best bits of anyone's training, life and racing. How often do you see 'aborted run at kilometre 11 because I had a dodgy stomach' or 'intervals were a nightmare today, legs felt like lead and called it a day before I did any more damage'. It does happen to the best runners, but it doesn't mean they're going to project that on Instagram. Cut yourself a wee break.

209. Post-race blues is a real thing; apparently something similar can happen after big occasions such as weddings or competing in the Olympics too. As a runner, you put huge amounts of time and energy, over a prolonged period, into one massive goal; when you achieve that goal it can be quite deflating, as that driven, focused part of your life is no longer there. Expect the blues post race and be prepared. Some find that planning the next goal, adventure or race keeps the post-race blues away, but remember you will often need some down time to recover, not just from the race, but from the block of training too.

210. If you do fail in achieving your goal, then it can be a lot less unsettling. The big goal is still there in the future and you still have your purpose so, ironically, you don't feel as down about it. Reflect, recover and, in time, you can try again.

211. Sometimes you might need a break from running, not just physically but mentally too, after an event. Take the time to do the things you might have abstained from in your preparation, like seeing non-running friends (remember them from the days you used to party every weekend?) or family, and doing some activities with your other half that don't totally revolve around your sport.

212. Look at seasonal and environmental factors too. Seasonal affective disorder, very effectively shortened to SAD, can affect people as the seasons change, due to changes in serotonin and melatonin levels in the body, so that could play a part in your lack of motivation.

213. General blood tests, either with your local doctor or a specialised online service such as Forth Edge or InsideTracker, might also reveal a deficiency that's affecting how you feel. If you're serious about your running, or just can't figure out why you're feeling rubbish all the time, it's worth making sure everything is in balance.

214. If you are having real trouble with your mental health then speak to someone: a friend, family member or a professional. It's something that affects a huge swathe of the population; and don't feel that you're not sad enough for it to count. If you're not your normal self, then there could be a reason and help could be just around the corner.

Running with friends is great, but running with your dog is better.   © Robbie Britton

TRAINING (73-287)

REST DAYS (215-223)

215. Stress plus rest equals growth. Without rest and recovery we simply don't improve so it's important to take it seriously, or at least consider rest and recovery when building your own training plan.

216. Having a regular rest day or two, normally Monday and Friday, works for many. On Monday you're recovering from the weekend and work is normally busy anyway, plus Friday lets you get ready for a bigger weekend of training.

217. Rest is different for everyone too. For some it's simply reducing their training down to a 30-minute run, some like to cross-train and others need a proper rest day and use the extra time for a nap (hardcore resting skills).

218. Work and travel come into play too. If you have the busiest day of the week or a long commute every Monday, it might seem smart to put that as your rest day, but is it really restful? If you feel a little extra bounce in your step on Tuesday, this is a good sign.

219. Your resting heart rate in the morning or heart rate variability can be a good objective measure of whether you need a day off or should be training. There are some good apps that do this measurement via the phone's camera and they can be accurate. The best apps also ask for qualitative data, such as your mood and energy levels, to provide a more holistic overview. However, don't be a total slave to technology in terms of when you should or shouldn't train. Some days an app will tell you that you are overtraining when you feel great, others it'll say you're not doing enough when you feel proper knackered. These apps are built to use algorithms based on large-scale data and studies and really can't take your entire life into account.

220. It can help to think of the 30 to 60 minutes which you might have used for running that day as an opportunity for rest. Hide away with a book, take a nap, do some yoga or try some meditation. Realistically, I know that not many people will get away with telling the family that they have to meditate on their rest day, but just try not to spend the whole 24 hours chopping wood or climbing up and down ladders. Unless it's your job of course – bosses don't take kindly to absconding from physical labour on rest days.

221. Cross-training on rest days can be useful if you still want to get out and about. Something low-impact, such as swimming or cycling, can actually boost recovery if you're just going easy and getting the blood flowing through the muscles.

222. This does not include HIIT classes and CrossFit. They are not restful. Have you seen the Murph workout in the CrossFit Games where participants have to run a mile and complete various other exercises? It's very entertaining, but not for the reasons they hope.

223. If you're not a fan of rest days, then at least look at the gaps between sessions and utilise those. You could run on a Sunday morning and then not again until Monday night and you'll at least have 30 hours between workouts. Rest days don't bite though, so don't be too scared.

TAPERING (224–245)

224. In the build-up to any key event the taper is one of the most important parts of your training. There are plenty of people who reckon that it doesn't work for them or they race best without one, but one could argue they've just not got it right yet.

225. A taper is a reduction in volume, while maintaining intensity and frequency of your runs. Its purpose is to maintain your hard-earned fitness and allow enough recovery to perform at your best on race day.

226. A common error is for athletes to increase the intensity or pace of their training runs in the taper, as they're feeling fresher, but this can be a mistake. You feel great, so instead of a controlled workout around your marathon pace, you push hard and smash out something closer to 5K pace and you're still recovering from that workout on race day.

227. The taper is the time to allow the hard work of the months and weeks beforehand to rise to the top, not to cram in extra training and drastically improve your fitness. Your fitness and performance will improve in your taper, not from working hard, but from recovering.

228. With frequency, if you normally run five times a week then it's okay to keep those normal runs in there, maybe add one extra rest day, but make each run a bit smaller to reduce the overall volume.

229. It's good to tap into your race pace during your taper week. Your body should be comfortable at this pace by now and a controlled workout, with short recoveries, can be a good confidence booster while keeping you sharp and preventing any detraining.

When in a pack, try not to spread across the whole path. Or just go at 5.00 a.m. © Tim Lloyd

Don't forget to smile – parkrun photographers will love you for it.   © *Pete Aylward, RunPhoto*

230. If the week progresses and you feel like an extra rest day is needed for your taper, then take it. I always remind ultra-runners that Bruce Fordyce, nine times winner of the Comrades Marathon, routinely took three whole days off in the build-up to race day.

231. The longer your race, the more important being fully rested on the start line becomes. At the faster end you want to be rested but still razor sharp, but in an ultra-marathon it's better to err on the side of caution and be at 95 per cent than to aim for 99 or 100 per cent and turn up a couple of per cent overcooked (or under-rested).

232. Experiment with what works for you and take notes. People do react to tapers differently and this can be down to a number of factors. These include, but aren't limited to, confidence, carb-loading and diet, day-to-day stress and previous experience.

233. In one of my favourite reviews of tapering studies (from Laurent Bosquet and his team back in 2007), eight to ten days was highlighted as an optimal time to taper for a runner, which allowed for extensive recovery but prevented detraining.

234. That said, you'll likely be building down from your peak training at least three or four weeks before your event, but not fully tapering yet.

235. When building your taper, and your overall training plan, think about the time needed to recover from each session and aim for that to have, theoretically, taken place before race day. Equally, remember that the impact of any one session takes time to sink in, so don't go looking for big improvements in those eight to ten days anyway.

236. If you include strength and conditioning in your training plan, then take this into account in your taper too. You can start to lose strength gains quite quickly but switching to a phase of 'maintenance' can be sensible in your last few weeks.

237. Take wider life into account in your taper too. If you're simply filling the extra time in with more work or a load of DIY chores, then you're missing the point of the taper a little.

238. If you normally include a fair amount of downhill running, then consider easing back on that in the week of the race as it can be most impactful in terms of training load.

239. When carb-loading in your taper, if you've planned well, the reduction in training should allow you to keep a normal diet, but still load glycogen stores, as you're not using as much energy as you usually would.

240. Still, some don't find the taper works for them due to an excessive increase in weight in this week or fort-night of tapering. All you should need to do is carefully consider your energy requirements during the taper. As mentioned in *tip 239*, if you're reducing overall workload then you might not need to put in a set carb-loading phase, and this could be part of your problem with tapering.

241. Be aware of taperitis. It's real. In the weeks before your race it is perfectly natural for pre-race anxiety and nerves to build and with more time on your hands in the taper, you must trust in the theory and recovery process, rather than working hard to get there.

242. Pre-race nerves are normal; they show that you care about your performance. The key balance is to make sure that anxiety does not outweigh excitement. The race is the reward for all your hard work and the thought of it should still make you smile, in between panics about missing your alarm on race day.

243. If you find you work best on a small taper, then it is okay to stick with it. Just don't write off tapering as garbage, as it does work when done correctly and you might be able to tinker a wee bit and improve your PB.

244. If you're routinely disappointed on race day, especially with a tired-feeling and slower second half of your race, then it could be down to the training and your taper. It's that or you need to work on fuelling *(tips 426–474)* or mental techniques *(tips 596–620)*.

245. A day of travelling or flights doesn't really count as a rest day. If you're simply without time to run, then you might still need a rest day in your taper. For some it's better to loosen the legs with a 30-minute easy run and some strides on a travel day and then have a proper rest the day before or after.

CROSS-TRAINING (246–256)

246. Cross-training is when you do another sport entirely, as a supplement to or replacement of your running. It can be when suffering or recovering from injury or as an add-on and can be a great way to increase training volume if you can't handle more running.

247. If you're only running three or four times a week and not suffering injury from the amount you're doing, then consider adding in some extra 30- or 45-minute easy runs into your week before you go straight on to a bike or cross-trainer, as more running will often be the best way to improve.

248. If you're reaching the limit of what your body can cope with then think about why this is, what you could do to improve it and if some additional cross-training could serve a purpose. Additional volume just for the sake of it isn't necessarily worthwhile.

249. When building back up from injury or time off, then using a bike, or another low-impact sport such as cross-country skiing, ski-mountaineering, swimming, rowing or a cross-trainer, can be a good way to increase your cardiovascular workout without overdoing it too soon.

250. Take care not to create an extra issue if you jump on a bike when injured. If, while trying to diagnose a running injury with your physio, you're creating a myriad of other issues with a poorly fitting bike, for example, then you might be off running for longer than you would have been without the cycling. Not that I'm talking from experience, I'm way too smart for that …

251. If you do enjoy a different sport then it can be a really good break, both physically and mentally, but think about how it impacts your running. I used to love a game of five-a-side football, but the odd ankle injury kept taking me away from my running training, so I had to evaluate which I was more focused on.

252. An off-season can be a good time to utilise your other hobbies. Time off running might be hard for you, but if you're cycling or cross-country skiing during that time then you're resting from the impact of running and doing something else you love. Until you fall over. I find using my face to take the brunt of any impact does reduce time off running, but mine already has quite a few scars.

Runners are notoriously bad at the YMCA dance. © Tim Lloyd

253. If you're getting on a bike, don't just double the time of your runs. There's a *1001 Tips* out there on how to make the most of your bike training; you can generally get more out of a lower-impact sport, especially in terms of volume, but make sure that you build up to it.

254. If you are doing a huge amount of cycling and swimming in addition to running, it's important to check you're not becoming a triathlete. Equally, if you try cross-country skiing and start shooting rifles, you might be a biathlete. The first step is admitting it.

255. Think outside the box. Bouldering could be a great way to get some core work in, snowshoeing could be an additional workout on the family skiing holiday and shuffle dancing was a key part of Dan Lawson's Land's End to John o' Groats (LEJOG) record. Well, he started doing two hours plus a day, so we had to take it into account at least. God only knows if it helped.

256. Enjoying something is a good enough reason to do an additional sport. As is doing a sport with friends. Staying social is important, especially if you're recently become this uber-runner and all your old pub or school friends are wondering where 'Robbie the Baby Rhino' went.

STRENGTH AND CONDITIONING* (257–287)

257. If you are doing more strength and conditioning workouts than actual running, then you are a cross-fitter and need to find *1001 Cross-Fit Tips*.

258. S&C (as the cool kids call it and as we shall going forward) is a supplementary part of your training. It's an additional aspect to running but the first S&C workout you do is the thousands of single leg movements combined into one workout: the run.

* Thank you to Sarah Tunstall, my physiotherapist and GB mountain runner, for her help with this section.

Douglas Samson concentrating on a tricky bit of trail above Loch Oss in the Tyndrum Hills. © Keri Wallace, Girls on Hills – *www.girlsonhills.com*

259. When starting out there are certainly some great exercises you can do to help with your running, especially if you're prone to injury. However, if you're struggling to find time to run but can do four body pump classes a week then it might be worth thinking about your priorities.

260. An elite runner might train anywhere from 10 to 16 hours a week and some of those will be supplementary sessions such as S&C. If a full-time athlete is getting two hours of S&C alongside 10 to 12 hours of running, then if you're running four or five hours a week it might be worth adjusting accordingly.

261. As little as two 20-minute S&C workouts per week can help injury-proof your running and have a beneficial effect on your performance if done correctly.

262. A common misconception is that you need to do lots of repetitions with small weights to train muscular endurance, but that's just what you're doing on each run. You might start out with a higher number of reps on certain exercises, but that's more about building capacity than endurance.

263. Before diving straight into heavier weights and bigger exercises (here's looking at the dudes in the room), it's important to work on two things: form and capacity.

264. Firstly form. If you're not doing a movement properly then you're likely not going to get the benefits and adaptations you're looking for. Worse still you might injure yourself or stress your body in a way that will develop into an injury in the future.

265. The best thing to do is work with a qualified S&C coach, preferably one with an interest in endurance sport, even if it's just for a couple of sessions, to get started correctly and work on your form. In reality, you might find that working with them longer term makes a whole lot of sense.

266. Recommendations from other athletes are often a good place to start, as well as the UK Strength and Conditioning Association. Make sure that you do your research and don't simply be swayed by a swishy Instagram page and rock-hard abs. This is where managing capacity comes in too. Not undertaking too much more than your body is capable of is key when building capacity.

267. The internet is wonderful, for many reasons, and you can find a whole bundle of steroid-filled chaps lifting big, heavy weights on YouTube. Eddie Hall lifting a 500-kilogram deadlift with blood starting to come out of every orifice might have 21 million views, but it might not be the best example of form for you starting out.

268. Look for videos of people who explain what they're doing and why, as it shows they have a deeper understanding of the exercise they're demonstrating. Ideally it should be advice from a registered professional so do check the credentials of any video you find as all sorts of weird and wonderful exercises can crop up on the internet. A video should also show various key angles too: front, side and rear.

269. Start with just your bodyweight until you get the form of the movements under control; don't skip straight to the hardest phase, as many runners like to do, without mastering the foundations. If you're struggling to do an exercise slowly and in a controlled manner without any additional weight, then introducing more weight is asking for trouble and will reinforce poor form.

270. The next step after simple bodyweight movements can simply be to slow those movements down, especially in the loading of the weight on to your muscle (the eccentric phase). Squats, lunges and press-ups become a whole different challenge when you go from one second to three seconds for the descent.

271. 'Eccentric' movements are not unconventional or in any way peculiar exercises that you need to perform – it just means lengthening of the muscle under load. This is often an area where runners suffer strength deficits and can sustain injuries, for example running downhill where the quadricep muscles on the front of the thigh need to act against the load of gravity in a lengthened position.

272. Try to film yourself from different angles (or ask a good friend or partner to) as it can show you areas you can improve in terms of form. That's actually what those massive selfie mirrors in the gym are for, believe it or not.

273. When starting out, expect some DOMS. This means delayed onset muscle soreness; 'delayed' means it can happen more than 24 hours after your workout so don't be too surprised.

274. A very basic rule of thumb: if both legs are sore in the same place they just need time to recover; if one leg is worse than the other or only one hurts, then it could be signs of an imbalance or injury. Both legs good (ish), one leg bad.

275. When adding S&C to your training plan, think about where it can go without having a massive impact on your running training. If you have to take four days off running with DOMS then maybe, just maybe, you're lifting too much.

276. Remember the soreness from DOMS will settle down as you adjust to the different exercises and become stronger.

277. The following three approaches to take are all different and can depend on your experience and lifestyle. It's okay to experiment with what works best for you; this might change throughout the year.

TRAINING (73-287)

278. First is to do your S&C on easy running days but making sure it's far enough away from any harder workouts so it won't impact on them. If you do S&C on a Tuesday evening then you might need to wait until Wednesday evening or Thursday morning to do your intervals.

279. Second is doing your S&C on the same day as your harder workouts. The logic being that you'll be recovering from both over the same time frame. Ideally you'll do your running workout first, so as to not impact on the main focus of your training. Then after a few hours, or in the evening, you do an S&C workout, taking into account the fatigue from your run, and then take it easy for the next couple of days.

280. Third is to split the S&C down into smaller component parts and 'micro-dose' it throughout the week. The aim is to get to a point where the stress on the body is small enough so that you can train well the next day; this is achieved by doing a few smaller additional workouts throughout the week, even just tagged on to the end of run sessions. This might be better suited to a maintenance phase of S&C training.

281. Talking of phases, the three main ones I would think about (remember I am not a qualified S&C coach, just a keen hobbyist) are capacity building, strength building and maintenance.

282. You build your capacity to undertake the exercises, normally through slightly higher reps than the strength workouts and lighter weights. You're making sure your form is good and your muscles are ready for the bigger workouts to come. This phase may also be used by your physiotherapist for rehabilitation purposes after an injury, to help load tendons and regain strength before returning to running.

283. Strength building is just that. You're building the strength of the muscles, not the size of them. Weights get heavier and the number of reps goes down. I'm wary of writing actual numbers in these sections as this isn't an S&C guide, but tips for those who should then go on to do some more research themselves.

284. Maintenance is holding on to your new strength at times when you aren't focusing as heavily on improving it. During peak volume training weeks or during tapers and race season you might just be avoiding the loss of strength, and this can be a lot less taxing on the body during those times.

285. Don't do a massive strength workout in the same week as your race. It feels like an obvious one, but for some it clearly isn't. When tapering you don't want to do anything that you'll still be recovering from on race day. Even if you've done enough S&C so that it doesn't make you sore any more, you may still fatigue large muscle groups that you need to run to your full potential.

286. Doing S&C won't bulk you up like Arnold Schwarzenegger. Do it right, and you can build strength without additional mass or even achieve a change in body composition that relates to improved performance. Even bodybuilders and powerlifters have very different training regimes; you need to do specific work to build massive muscles. Just stop eating rare steaks and raw eggs after those workouts.

287. The good news about S&C is that when it is done correctly, running will gradually help to reinforce your newly gained strength. The S&C exercises should be designed to translate to a stronger and more efficient running form which is then practised repeatedly within the running gait cycle to reinforce the movement pattern and reduce injury risk.

Nicola Redgewell takes on the Devil's Ridge, Scottish Highlands.   © *Keri Wallace, Girls on Hills – www.girlsonhills.com*

You can tell which of these runners only races on the track for 24 hours at a time.   © *Tim Lloyd*

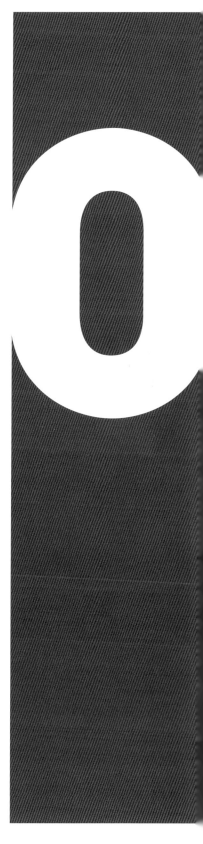

Navigating using a map is a great skill to have (*tip 328*) – here Lorna MacInnes sets the map on Buachaille Etive Beag, Glen Coe.
© Keri Wallace, Girls on Hills – *www.girlsonhills.com*

003

SKILLS AND
TECHNIQUES
(288–339)

*'When you get to the top of the hill put in a little spurt
to get your legs moving a bit faster for the downhill.
Just enough to push you over the crest of the hill as the
gradient is likely to be easing off at this point anyway.'*

SKILLS AND TECHNIQUES (288–339)

DOWNHILL RUNNING (288–318)

288. Whether you prefer to run on roads or trails, you're going to encounter hills at some point so it's worth getting some specific practice in. In a race, they say you win it on the uphill, but you can lose it on the downhill.

289. Running down a road is mostly about the conditioning of your legs, trying to lean into the descent and not slamming on the brakes. It's not a technical skill like on the trails, but you can really tell if someone isn't used to it.

290. If there are just one or two short descents in your race then you can probably get away without much more conditioning. You'll trash your legs but, by the time this happens, hopefully your race is already over.

291. If you have a long descent or multiple significant ones, then your performance can be hindered if your legs aren't up to the task. Hobbling the last section of the race with smashed quads might be the difference between winning and losing.

292. Train specifically for your events, so if you have a hilly road race then simulate that in your training, at a similar pace or effort level to your race. It might slow down your averages to do your threshold run on a hilly country lane, but remember it's race day that really matters.

293. Continuous hills, or Kenyan hills (where you maintain a consistent effort while running downhill and uphill), can also be a useful session for conditioning your legs for the descents. Just make sure you respect the recovery if you're new to it *(tips 157–158)*.

294. If you know a downhill is coming and you're good at them, then it might be a good time to push away from a competitor; crest the hill with a few metres to spare and you might break their spirit a little.

295. A downhill on the road, and the trail for that matter, can be a time to recover while still moving fast. A relaxed, free-flowing stride downhill will mean you don't lose any ground but easing off the throttle a little can help recover for the next uphill.

296. On the trails, downhill running is one of the most technical elements of our sport. Rather than switching your brain off for the downhills and letting go, you need to do the opposite. Engage your brain; every downhill you run in training is a chance for some purposeful practice. Even the crazy paving on a friend's drive or a steep set of stairs is a chance to think about how you're moving.

297. I don't say this as a downhill maestro, more someone who was pretty rubbish at downhills who has built themselves up to a half-decent level and I think that leaves me in an okay place to help. Many of the top descenders have been crushing it down fells or mountainsides since they were knee high and it's second nature now. Someone who's had to try and build the skill as an adult has potentially had to think about it more, mainly because of fear.

298. It's more about being a wee bit outside your comfort zone and pushing ahead progressively than just going wild down as many hills as you can.

299. Slow down a little in training and try to think about how you move. It's braking that does the most damage so if you're hammering down fast you might get to the bottom of the hill quickly, but at a very high cost. The second descent in your race will hurt even more and in an ultra you might not make the finish.

Loose, rocky ground on the Lavaredo Ultra Trail, Italy. © Pete Aylward, RunPhoto

300. Slow down and you have more time to interpret what is in front of you. Your brain, with practice, will gather the information it sees ahead of you together and you'll start to move with more fluidity. Instead of seeing each individual rock and how to get round it, you'll start to plan a series of movements for the steps ahead, like a chess Grandmaster. They're not thinking one pawn at a time, that's for sure.

301. Physically find out what works for you. Experiment. Smaller, fast steps can reduce the impact, but might also limit how you go round certain obstacles; this might also change with the technicality of the ground in front of you.

302. Wide arms and a low centre of gravity can help with balance. Pretend you're an aeroplane flying down the hill. Aeroplane noises optional, but don't let anyone tell you that you can't.

303. Research the kind of terrain you'll be racing on and try to practise on similar ground. If you want to get super geeky then think about the geology too. Certain rocks are grippier than others; practising on Peak District gritstone is totally different to slate in Snowdonia and the limestone and granite in the Alps.

304. Even if you live somewhere flatter, just find yourself a short piece of technical trail to practise your drills on. Don't make it all about speed though, as efficiency is your friend the longer your race is.

305. Even going over the same technical trail three or four times, you will see improvements. Being slightly outside your comfort zone will see that zone expand and then you just keep pushing one or two per cent each time and your ability and confidence will both grow.

306. Look at the lines the water takes if it's created runnels; it will flow down the best route, but that's not always directly down the hill.

307. When you're going into bends and zigzags you want to avoid slamming on the brakes and smashing those quads. Either adopt a slower pace so you can hold it round the bend more easily, or ease back when you see the bend coming and try to exit the turn at the same pace, or faster, than you entered it.

308. Try slowing down a little so you can avoid twisting and turning around rocks and obstacles, taking a more direct line. It might be slower running, but a quicker route, so you'll get to the bottom of the hill quicker. The more in control you are, the easier it is to pick the path of least resistance.

309. Keep your eyes on the trail ahead, not on the floor right in front of you. The better you can be at interpreting the challenges ahead, the quicker you can go. This can be harder at night, so it's worth slowing a tiny bit as your brain will have more information to take in with less light.

SKILLS AND TECHNIQUES (288–339)

310. If your race involves you descending at night then practise descending in the night. Simples.

311. If you're fortunate enough to have friends who are quick downhill then observe them to improve your own descending. Think about what they're doing too; if they're just faster and going hard downhill, but smashing themselves to do so, it might not be best for you.

312. Some of the best ultra-marathon runners are so accomplished at running downhill that it's actually a bit of a recovery for them. They're still going fast, but not all out, and at a level that helps them recover from the previous hard uphill.

313. If you're someone who overtakes lots of people downhill, ask yourself how much of this is because you're just a better downhill runner and how much is that you're trying harder to make up for the previous climb. As the race progresses, those who are more relaxed on the downhills will get further away on each climb and you'll gain back less on each descent.

314. If you have a long descent, don't forget to eat. Just because your effort level is lower doesn't mean you can stop eating for the downhill. You're refuelling for the next climb and you might be able to digest a little better as you're not working as hard.

315. 'If you don't fall over every now and again then you're not trying hard enough' sounds good as a tip, but it's macho nonsense. Don't be put off by a fall either. Check you're okay, count your limbs and get back up into the action. The sooner you get going again the easier it is to get back your confidence.

316. If you bang your head then it's a different matter. You might have concussed yourself and if you lost consciousness at all then no race is worth that risk of falling and banging your head again as your cognitive functions may already be impaired. If you can get to a checkpoint then let them know you have banged your head, but if you need help then ask other runners. Most of them are good people (although some will buzz past) and they will help you.

317. If you see another runner fall and bang their head then please do stop and check they're alright. Even if they haven't bumped their head, check they're okay. Someone with a concussion can be confused and make poor decisions so it can be helpful to just keep an eye on them for a couple of minutes even if they insist that they are okay.

318. If someone asks for your help in a race, remember it's only a race and this is a fellow human being in need. Do the right thing.

UPHILL RUNNING OR HIKING (319–326)

319. At a certain pace it's more efficient to hike uphill than run. This might be different for different athletes, but it's worth thinking about it in your own training and racing. If someone walks past when you're running, that's generally an indicator that you'd be better off hiking.

320. If you're running uphill then think about it as going into the granny gear on your bike. Smaller steps, higher cadence (the number of steps you take per minute), eyes up the hill and arms driving. Keeping your eyes and chin up will keep your breathing more open too.

Run if you can, hike if you should and roll if you have to. © *Tim Lloyd*

321. If you like hiking then hopefully you've got the hiking poles already sorted *(tips 817–829)*, but the old-fashioned hands-on-knees or quads is always a good look. I've no idea if it's more effective than simply driving your arms, but you look the business. Think about where you place your hands – my favourite spot is just above the knee, on the vastus medialis. The bottom half of my leg is now my hiking pole.

322. When you get to the top of the hill put in a little spurt to get your legs moving a bit faster for the downhill. Just enough to push you over the crest of the hill as the gradient is likely to be easing off at this point anyway.

323. On a long uphill don't just get caught in an uphill stroll. Hike with purpose and if it flattens out a little bit then get those legs working again. Knowing when to hike and when to run is a skill that needs working on, and can be affected by gradient, terrain, heat, energy levels, altitude and just how your day is going.

324. Uphill racing is always going to make up a bigger part of your race than downhill, simply because it takes longer to travel five kilometres uphill than it does five kilometres downhill, so working on your uphill might bring the biggest gains.

325. If you're lucky enough to be able to do a long uphill run and to miss out the downhill, such as by taking a cable car in the Alps, then you get an awful lot of cardiovascular benefit for a much lower impact on the body. The damage of big vertical training weeks comes on the downhills so, when training in Chamonix, I would try to take out a few of those long descents.

326. If you're going to be hiking uphill in your race then practise this in your training; but I might have mentioned this already. Too often you see people inefficient and uncomfortable when they have to hike; most ultras and a lot of mountain, fell and trail races will have some power hiking in there.

NAVIGATION (327–339)

327. On the most basic level navigation is the art of knowing where you are and where you are going. It's worth learning some navigation skills – it's not just for the mountains, as you can use them on urban runs too.

328. Too often we rely on technological navigation aids – our watches, phone and GPS devices – but if these fail we're in trouble. You don't need to go everywhere holding a map and a thumb compass, but knowing how to use them is a really useful skill.

'Dan, why does it say we're near Bognor Regis now? I'll do the nav from now on.' © James Vincent

SKILLS AND TECHNIQUES (288–339)

329. We all use our own navigation skills day-to-day. Following the outside of a field to get round to the other side, pacing using a landmark in the distance or just using your phone to find an address. Trust in your own ability a wee bit.

330. Whether training or racing, if you're unsure on direction it's always worth slowing down a bit and making sure. In training you might end up lost or just make it a longer run, but it can be hugely demoralising to get lost in a race, even if only for a few minutes.

331. Sign up for a local orienteering event if you want to get better and learn how to navigate on the move. Orienteering communities are friendly; you'll get a good interval workout and improve your skills.

332. If you're heading into more remote countryside and mountains then it's really worth developing navigation skills as situations can get a lot more serious. There are some great companies out there, including NAV4 Adventure run by Joe Faulkner, who can teach you the basics or help you advance your skills.

333. Weather conditions and time of day can change the difficulty of navigation too, especially if visibility is affected. Not only does it stop you from using landmarks around you, but it also affects how fast you think you're moving.

334. For those uncertain with a map, but stuck in the middle of nowhere, 'handrailing' is a good technique. If you do find something you recognise on your map, such as a wall, road or fence, that you can follow, then 'handrail' along it. Sticking to something solid might be more effective than trying to save time cutting corners, even if you ended up going a little further to avoid getting lost.

335. In this day and age, you can't just follow other people's footsteps either. There are too many paragliders, base jumpers and wingsuiters around. Also they might just be going somewhere different to where you want to go.

336. If you are relying on a navigation device, then make sure you have enough juice. Power banks can be handy if you're on a long run. If you want to save on the weight and always have a backup, then consider using an older GPS device that is powered by AA batteries. You can carry one spare set with you and it's always easy enough to find a shop that sells AA batteries, unless you're really out in the wilds.

337. Learn about contour lines, whatever you're using to navigate. I won't name names, but on an adventurous trip with another runner he once asked me what all the lines meant on the map screen. Contour lines don't just tell you how steep a slope is, they can also help you understand where you are and where to go. Being able to place contour features you can see on the map in the landscape ahead of you is a skill that takes time to develop, but can be really useful.

338. Always be wary of allowing yourself to see what you want or expect to see, either in the landscape ahead or on the map. You could be looking for a certain hillock, stream or trail and come across something quite similar, but ultimately different, which can change your whole perspective of the map to suit what's in front of you.

339. Navigation is tough, especially if you're in a group and the others aren't doing their fair share. Ideally, share the workload, but if you can't, make sure the rest of the group appreciate that you're using more mental energy and are not as free to complete other tasks, such as fuelling and looking after yourself, as they are.

Looking ahead I could see Dan going the wrong way, but was excited for the rest I'd get waiting for him to come back on course.   © *James Vincent*

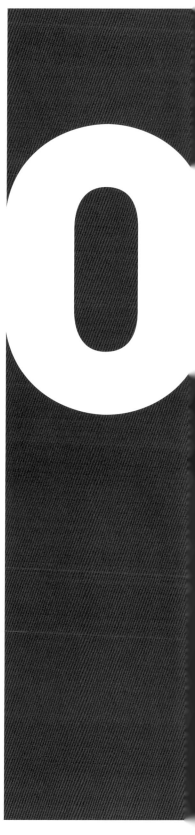

Running at Lake Baikal, Siberia, where it gets to -30 °C below and you want *everything* covered in order for it to stay attached long term. © Robbie Britton

004

ENVIRONMENT (340–402)

*'Gloves are great, but mittens are better. Keeping your fingers
in contact will mean they will generate more heat together.
It is, however, harder to take selfies.'*

A little-known fact about Dan Lawson is that his head isn't actually in the middle of his shoulders. © *James Vincent*

ENVIRONMENT (340-402)

HOT WEATHER (340-353)

340. The weather can stop plenty of new and old runners in their tracks, but a bit of preparation can help you deal with a whole host of adverse conditions. Typically, runners can cope with heat with physiological adaptations and the cold with technological (i.e. by using the right kit).

341. Acclimatising to the heat takes time; if you're racing somewhere hot it is certainly worth taking this into account. If you can get there 10 to 14 days before your event you will acclimatise to a good level, but this isn't possible for most of us.

342. The next best thing can be using a heat chamber to train in; these can often be found in university sports labs and can be hired out by the hour. Again, the 10 to 14 days before your event are key. An hour each day could make a big difference to how prepared your body is for the heat on race day.

343. Now we're going down the scale and we're at saunas. The goal of these methods is just to raise your body temperature each day and get some adaptation. It needs to be consistent, but if you can't visit a sauna or a heat chamber every day then an hour running in all your clothes will still get your core temperature up.

344. Last, and probably least, is having a hot bath for at least 20 minutes. Get a sweat on and, once again, get that core temperature up. Try not to pass out in the bath though.

345. One of our adaptations to heat is to start sweating earlier, as sweat makes it easier to dissipate heat from your wet skin through evaporation. So, if you're just really sweaty, you can tell your friends you're training for a race in the desert.

346. When doing heat training before an event make sure to adequately hydrate. There's no point in being better adapted to the heat if you're exhausted from the process of getting there. You're not a boxer trying to hit fighting weight, you are an endurance athlete, likely in a taper. Act accordingly.

347. If you are racing in the heat then try to target areas where blood flow is increased, such as your neck, scalp and wrists, with cold water and ice. The biggest differences have been shown with ingesting icy drinks, but there can be gastro-intestinal side effects and it is not always practical.

348. You can buy purpose-built neckerchiefs (old-school name for a Buff®, I think) or wrist pockets that are perfect for filling with ice. You can also make some yourself with a little bit of thread, a needle and some old sleeves.

349. In longer races, if you stop at a checkpoint, just to catch your breath, or to cool down, then make sure you're in the shade. Too often we stop, but still expose ourselves to the very thing that's making us so tired. This tip was taught to me by my dog Rosa, who would look at me with bemusement from the shade on hot days.

350. Different objects provide a different quality of shade, so a light tarpaulin roof at a checkpoint might not help much, but the shade of a building or big tree certainly will.

351. When running in the heat you do need to adapt your effort accordingly. Even those who are acclimatised have to run easier as the mercury rises. Heat calculators are available online, which take run intensity, humidity and temperature into account.

ENVIRONMENT (340-402)

352. In humid conditions your body loses some of its ability to cool down via sweating, so you can be even more vulnerable to heat exhaustion and should adjust effort levels accordingly.

353. Spending too much time in the heat can lead to heat exhaustion and sunstroke. Heat exhaustion means you'll feel dizzy, fatigued and nauseous. Your heart rate might be weak, but fast. Sunstroke is an extremely serious condition and requires medical treatment. You'll stop sweating, experience confusion and can lose consciousness; it can be fatal.

COLD WEATHER (354–367)

354. When the body gets too cold it reacts by drawing heat from the extremities to protect your core. The body is protecting the vital internal organs, but unhelpfully takes away your ability to use the things that will help you improve your own situation – your hands and feet. Best to not let it get that far.

355. With the cold it's not as much about adaptation, but equipment. Having said that, there are some interesting techniques used by 'The Iceman', Wim Hof, that might help, including breathing techniques and the benefits of continued exposure to cold temperatures; but this is more likely to create a beneficial psychological adaptation, rather than a physical one.

356. In cold conditions it's important to not to let yourself get too cold or too warm. It's a Goldilocks situation. If you get too hot then you sweat, which dampens your skin and clothes, which then wick away heat more quickly than they would otherwise. If you stop in the cold with wet clothes you will feel your temperature drop really quickly.

357. For a fast-moving, shorter race, where you know you'll be working hard the whole time, you might get away with this as you can change, as soon as you stop, into dry clothes.

358. If you're out for a longer period of time, have multiple checkpoints or know you'll be hiking or slowing down in the latter stages of your event, you need to plan accordingly. Think about your kit for when you're running, but also for when you're walking or stopped.

359. Be bold, start cold. This is one of my favourite tips for starting out on colder weather adventures. How you feel at the start of your run will change and you will heat up as the body starts working harder. If you're hot, or even 'just right' as you leave the door then you'll likely be too hot quite quickly.

360. Layering is the key; a windproof layer will go a long way in keeping the heat you create inside. Running in Arctic Sweden, with temperatures from -5 °C down to -23 °C, I had windproof trousers and a light windproof jacket on top of a merino base layer. Any more layers, and I was sweating as I moved and would get cold as soon as I stopped. This only worked as I was running for most of the event and had a down jacket to keep heat in should I need to.

361. It's a common misconception that most body heat is lost through our heads. A 1950s study on US soldiers claiming that the soldiers lost most of their body heat from their heads has since been debunked – they lost heat from their heads mainly because that was the only part of their skin exposed to the colder environment. If you're all wrapped up, but still wearing shorts, you will lose a lot of heat from your legs and, as a consequence, your whole system will be cooler.

A well-wrapped-up runner descending Aonach Beag in early winter conditions, Scottish Highlands. © *Keri Wallace, Girls on Hills* – *www.girlsonhills.com*

362. I often hear 'I'm okay in shorts because my legs are warm, but my hands are always cold'. See above. If you're losing heat from the biggest heat producers (your legs) then your body won't have as much to spare for the extremities. It's like complaining about a cold kitchen when you have the heating on full blast, but the back door is open.

363. Gloves are great, but mittens are better. Keeping your fingers in contact will mean they will generate more heat together. It is, however, harder to take selfies.

364. Windproof and waterproof over-gloves can be packed up pretty small, but have a really big impact when worn over your normal gloves in wilder conditions.

365. Want an extra, lightweight emergency pair of gloves? Disposable, latex gloves don't weigh a thing, will make your hands pretty sweaty, but will help keep them warm. It's a good emergency backup; the same can go for plastic booties (or two shower caps) to put between your socks and your shoes.

ENVIRONMENT (340-402)

Don't waste time dodging puddles, you'll get soaked eventually so embrace the splash. © Tim Lloyd

366. Feeling the cold and have no more clothes with you? Keep moving. The more heat you generate, the better, but ration it out if you have a long way to go because exhaustion in cold conditions can quickly become a bigger problem.

367. Keep the fuel going into the fire too, as you will burn more energy generating heat to keep yourself warm too. If your hands are cold, you're also likely to not eat as much, so keep food easy to reach and remind yourself on a regular basis to keep chomping down.

RAIN (368-381)

368. Running in the rain is good for the soul, especially if it's wet and warm. Don't be put off by a spot of precipitation – get out there and smile.

369. If it's patchy weather, just short bursts of rainfall, then think about clothes and shoes that dry and drain quickly. Thicker materials hold more water and can weigh you down after the showers have stopped.

370. The best way to stay dry is to stay indoors, which is no fun. Second best is an umbrella, but they're hard to run with. Next we have waterproof jackets. The balance between a jacket that keeps water out, but is breathable enough that you don't drown in your own sweat, is an art, not a science.

371. A waterproof jacket without (and even with) a hood isn't waterproof. There's a hole where your head comes out and water goes in. The same could be said for waterproof socks and shoes when worn with shorts.

372. The lighter weight a waterproof jacket is, the less likely it is to be useful in actual rainstorms. If you really need to stay dry and will be out in bad weather for an extended period of time, then go for a decent, multi-layered material such as GORE-TEX PRO. It will be heavier and less breathable, so you'll need to adjust your effort to stop you soaking yourself underneath and defeating the object of the jacket in the first place.

373. A newer style of waterproof material from some brands has no outer membrane, so it's a lot lighter, more breathable and the beads of water can literally be shaken off. In terms of waterproofing and breathability, it's second to none, but longevity and wearing with a pack are impacted, so you might need to re-waterproof a little more often.

374. If you're going to be running with a pack, think about getting a slightly larger jacket so you can put your jacket on over both you and your running vest. Not only will this be simpler, quicker and keep everything dry, some jacket materials aren't built to have anything in contact with them and will delaminate rather quickly.

375. If you're running for more than one day in the rain, then you have to look after your feet. Changing into fresh socks can be as good as a new pair of shoes, for about twenty minutes at least. Dry your feet with a towel or cloth and even consider using talcum powder to put on your feet and in the sock as it will soak up extra moisture.

376. There are fancy gadgets to dry your shoes; yesterday's newspaper does a good job too. Take out the insole to dry next to the shoe and stuff your preferred tabloid in there. Try to sort it so that someone's face is looking out at you from the shoe, and it'll make you smile before your next run.

377. A waterproof hat is more useful than you might first imagine. After finding one on a trail once, I now quite like using mine.

378. The same goes for waterproof shorts. Initially I thought they'd just be too sweaty and I didn't see the point. If you need to keep your legs dry, then use your waterproof trousers. But when your jacket, if working properly, beads all the water down on to your legs, waterproof or water-resistant shorts will hopefully keep the liquid flowing towards the ground. It might be too hot for waterproof trousers, but you still don't want a soaked crotch.

379. Carefully consider your shoe choice when it's raining. Usually safe trails can become slippery, chalk can become like ice and a sharp tarmac bend, in shoes with shoddy grip, can see you hit the deck. Stay rubber-side down as much as possible.

380. Waterproof shoes are similar to the jacket without a hood – flawed. They keep you dry for the first few puddles, but, without a waterproof gaiter or trousers to keep the rain from entering at the top, you'll get wet and then the waterproofing will keep the water inside instead.

381. The exception is in snowy conditions. Your feet come into contact with the snow on the ground and that can soak through normal shoes, but waterproof shoes will keep your feet dry. The other option in this situation is waterproof socks.

ENVIRONMENT (340-402)

ALTITUDE (382-402)

382. Here's some science for you – when you get closer to outer space the atmospheric pressure is lower which means it's harder for your body to access the available oxygen in the air. We use a fair amount of oxygen, especially when running harder, so the higher you go, the harder it is to run at your normal pace. This should, over time, trigger an increase in red blood cells and increase your ability to deliver oxygen to your muscles, but not immediately to help you on that particular run.

383. Adjust your effort accordingly when above sea level. Below 900 or 1,000 metres, you might not feel too much difference, although it can be noticeable at a lower level than this for some.

384. The worthwhile altitude training barrier most suggest is 1,600 to 1,800 metres above sea level. Traditional European altitude training areas such as Font Romeu and St Moritz are above this level. Popular locations outside Europe, such as Iten, Kenya (2,400 metres) and Flagstaff, Arizona (2,100 metres), are even higher.

385. Keep in mind that the scientific evidence behind the effectiveness of altitude training for performance at sea level is still not conclusive. You certainly acclimatise to running at higher altitudes by gaining more red blood cells, but differentiating this from the benefits of simply training in a group or being on a training camp is not easy.

386. If you are looking to use altitude in your training then know that the minimum amount of time for it to be beneficial is considered to be three weeks, with the first week giving time to adapt initially to a harder work rate.

387. One of the negative aspects of altitude training is the need to work at a lower speed to achieve the same intensity. This is why some will 'live high, train low'; for example Lac de Matemale is near to Font Romeu but is a few hundred metres lower and is used by athletes for threshold and faster efforts.

388. You really have to be at altitude for more than 18 hours per day for the benefits to be useful, so methods such as sleeping or training in an altitude tent are not likely to provide the results you're after.

389. With altitude tents you also need to take into account the chance that it can interfere with one of the most important parts of your training – sleep. Having tested one myself, the dreams I had over the first couple of nights made me feel like I was on an acid trip, but that could have just been me.

390. Altitude tents also require the agreement of your significant other – it's probably best not to invest in one before asking if your other half wants to go on an extended camping trip in their own home. There are places you can rent them from, which is cheaper, especially if it has to go back again.

391. Wearing one of those strange face masks won't simulate altitude training, it'll just make you breath harder. Save your cash and just try breathing through a straw for a run. You'll still look less stupid.

392. With altitude training, it is also about a cumulative build-up over time, without extended trips back to sea level. Anyway, if you're reading this to help improve your parkrun time, we're getting ahead of ourselves anyway. Warm weather training is a much better bet first.

393. If you're racing at altitude then there are two main things to consider: how it will affect your performance and if you need to consider acclimatisation for health and safety.

British ultra-runner Sophie Grant on a stunning bit of trail in the Dolomites. © Pete Aylward, RunPhoto

394. For serious altitude, that is going above 2,500 metres, especially for extended periods of time, you have to start considering altitude sickness and this is beyond the remit of this book. I'll try to point you in the right direction.

395. Altitude acclimatisation takes time. You go higher for a bit, come back down to recover and then go higher again. It can take days or weeks, depending on how high you're going, but the consequences of ignoring it are huge. High-altitude pulmonary oedema and high-altitude cerebral oedema can kill you.

396. While a couple of visits to an altitude chamber before your trip likely won't make a huge physiological difference it can help you prepare psychologically. Get used to what it will feel like higher up before you get there, and you'll be better able to deal with it more effectively in reality.

397. When racing at mountain events that go up high or shorter races that start and finish above 2,000 metres you can either get there 10 to 12 days beforehand and hope to do some acclimatisation or there are suggestions that arriving quite shortly before the race itself will avoid the side effects of the altitude kicking in before you run. Obviously, the former makes more sense, but it's not an option open to all.

398. Notice how you react to altitude and adapt your plans accordingly. If you felt sick the day before your race and you're heading back next year, then it could be worth changing your plans around a bit next time.

399. Some experience nausea and sickness as they get higher, which is often linked to dehydration too. Take care to plan your nutrition and hydration with this in mind. In a mountain race you might only be popping up to a significant height for a short time, but if you're stopped from eating and drinking due to nausea then it can have a big impact on the rest of your race. You want to have the energy to enjoy that downhill.

400. Expect the tougher times too. Too often I see people complain about it 'not being their day' or 'not feeling right from the start' in a race that goes up high and they haven't realised it's the same for 99 per cent of the starting field (exceptions being high-altitude natives such as Columbians and Kenyans, or Kilian Jornet).

401. Look at your race profile and take into account when you'll be at higher elevations. Make sure you fuel up well before you get to these points, just in case you struggle to eat and drink, and then slow down a bit accordingly. Don't hammer yourself when the cost is higher due to the lack of oxygen.

402. Take even more extra care when altitude is combined with heat. That'll really knock your socks off if you're not careful.

Working with others in training will drive you harder, just don't do it on every run. © Tim Lloyd

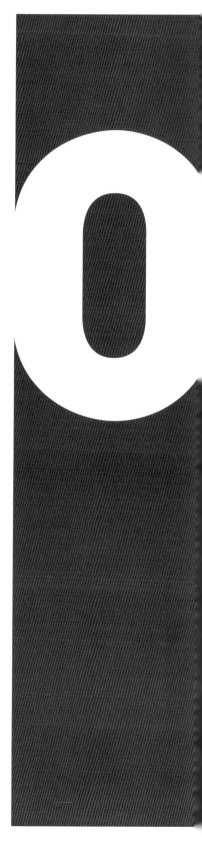

Robbie actually swallowed the phone shortly after the gel. © *James Vincent*

005

THE RUNNER'S BODY (403–554)

'Put the same effort into eating as you do to driving your legs forward. When you're struggling to get to the next lamp post ahead, but using all your will to keep pushing, remember you could have avoided running out of energy by putting that same effort level into eating an energy gel that was a bit too sickly.'

THE RUNNER'S BODY (403-554)

NUTRITION (403-425)

403. Nutrition is a subject that many would have you believe is super complicated, but it's not. It can be complex, but, for the most part, it doesn't have to be. There are fundamental basics that you need to get right, like having enough energy to fuel your run, which many people seem to miss from the start.

404. If your main goal from reading this book is to improve your nutrition, then there are more detailed books and resources for this purpose, Renee McGregor's *Fast Fuel: Food for Running Success* being one of them. I've studied the two-year postgraduate IOC Diploma in Sports Nutrition; my main focus is race nutrition, rather than day-to-day nutrition, so that's what I'll focus on here.

405. Anyone who suggests that their keto, plant-based or banana-only diet is the answer to all humankind's woes should be viewed sceptically. Watch out for one-size-fits-all solutions and people that write in CAPITAL LETTERS ON SOCIAL MEDIA ABOUT THEIR DIET.

406. A healthy, balanced diet, with a mixture of macro-nutrients and micronutrients, is a good thing. Your body needs carbohydrates, fats and proteins to do different jobs, possibly at different times; more on that later.

407. Skinny and lighter doesn't automatically mean faster, but there is a relationship between lower body fat and performance. It's not never-ending and it's very individual and gender-specific too, so don't just think that you need to strip all the fat off your body to go as fast as possible. It can also go too far and become detrimental to your running and general health.

408. Finding the right level for yourself can involve some experimenting with different race weights, working with a professional dietician and making some mistakes, but factors such as long-term health and consistency need to come into play too.

409. If you're so lean that you are constantly ill, tired and angry, then you're not going to be training to your full potential. That's before even getting to the stage where you develop vitamin deficiencies and poor bone health.

410. Periodise your nutrition, taking the same approach to the chaos of periodisation *(tips 184–197)*, and think about the fuel you need at any one time.

411. Be it making sure you have sufficient muscle glycogen stores for your midweek session, ingesting a 15- or 20-gram dose of protein after you've worked your muscles in the gym or the track, or even taking a vitamin D supplement during the winter months, try to think about making your nutrition right for you, at different stages of your training.

412. Having some simple go-to snacks for after hard sessions can be great, especially if they tick the protein and carbo-hydrate boxes when you need to. There are good ready-made or home-made options, or simply a glass of chocolate milk.

413. Don't take supplements just because you think you're covering all the bases. If you have an insufficiency which is difficult to improve with your diet, such as vitamin D in the winter, then it might be worthwhile, but taking multivitamins year-round just in case could simply be making your wee more nutrient-dense and could also overload certain areas.

Live to eat or eat to live? Maybe it's just 'eat to run hundreds of miles in one go'. © *James Vincent*

414. RED-S (relative energy deficiency in sport) is a real problem in endurance sport, and on a very basic level is a prolonged period of taking in less energy than you're burning. For female athletes your menstrual cycle is an in-built warning system for RED-S; if you're missing periods or having irregular periods then that can be a sign of bigger problems. Talk to your GP or a specialist dietician and don't be brushed off with 'that's just normal for someone training at your level'. It isn't.

415. Men can also fall foul of this severe imbalance in energy, but don't have as obvious an indicator. Some suggest that lack of a morning erection and low libido can be a sign of RED-S in male athletes, so make sure your pecker is behaving normally.

416. Other symptoms or impacts of RED-S can be increased irritability, depression and injury risk or decreased perform-ance, strength, concentration and bone health. For more information, the IOC Consensus Statement is often a good place to start, with academics including Kirsty Elliott-Sale, Margo Mountjoy and Louise Burke behind important research on this subject.

417. If you think you might be falling foul of under-fuelling your training and lifestyle in general, as it's not as simple as eating what you burn in your sessions, then please do some-thing about it before it becomes a chronic issue. It's most likely not just a simple imbalance of input and output, but a mix of psychological aspects too, which can take time to work on.

418. Your nutrition and energy demands are dynamic. They change over time and it's important to consider this.

419. On a day-to-day basis a female athlete will experience changes in their energy demands and usage alongside their menstrual cycle, with their bodies utilising different substrates in different phases. This is under-researched and very individual; keeping a diary of your own cycle and symptoms can help increase your understanding of your own cycle and needs.

420. Athletes in general will see their own dietary needs change throughout a season, with demands around heavy training, increased strength work or racing all potentially needing different adaptions to their diet.

421. As with anything, if you want to know more than utilise the internet. There are so many resources out there, but, with nutrition more than most subjects, don't take everything at face value. Look for reputable, evidence-based advice and don't be afraid to question something you either don't understand, or disagree with.

422. Consider your sources. The IOC Consensus Statements, meta-analysis or reviews are the top tier, as they take in a huge amount of research and draw conclusions based on a large body of evidence. Some chap on Twitter might have lost 10 kilograms on a diet of house bricks alone, but aside from this being a case study of one, it's also not a scientific experiment that considers all the factors. He might have lost his arm, which could have accounted for eight of those kilograms, or he simply gave up drinking beer at the same time.

423. Any improvements down to extreme diet can often be explained by a sudden weight loss, often from excluding certain foods that were a staple of the diet beforehand. It doesn't mean that diet is a super solution for everyone; the long-term sustainability of the diet, the weight loss and your health should be considered.

424. Day-to-day nutrition isn't simply a physiological science or equation, but psychological too. Knowing exactly the right foods to eat for optimum performance doesn't mean that you will eat them; trying to look at it from a psychological angle will help too. For example, I might have an excellent nutrition plan for my week, with periodised carbohydrate intake around my bigger sessions, but then my budgie dies, I want some comfort food and before I know it there's an empty bag of Haribo next to me. It's not the end of the world and you can adapt around life, as now I'm probably well fuelled for that night's progression workout, but knowing how to adapt, and understanding that life isn't as simple as a nutrition plan or spreadsheet would want, is key.

425. There are no such things as 'superfoods', except for a bag of Haribo Tangfastics at mile 80 of a 100-mile race.

PRE-RACE FOOD (426–442)

426. If you're falling apart in the latter stages of races, especially the marathon, it could likely be down to your fuelling. Or your pacing. Probably both, as they're linked.

427. The fuel we use when we run is influenced by the intensity at which we're running and this in turn can be influenced by our training, diet and some other factors too. So don't just think about fuelling as 'how many energy gels I eat per hour'.

428. The main sources of fuel for running are body fat stores, body glycogen stores (in your muscles and liver) and the carbohydrates we chuck in before and during our running. We have a much greater ability to store body fat, but it's not our body's go-to energy source when we're running, especially as we start to work harder.

429. Before a race, or a harder session, we can pre-load our muscles with more glycogen, which is often called carb-loading. It's basically like storing extra energy gels in your muscles and liver for when you need them.

430. Practise your carb-loading before race day. Every long run, especially those where you have race-specific blocks, is a chance to see what works for you. The guidelines in the next few tips may need some tinkering and/or training to be right for you and your gut.

431. In terms of carb-loading we need to bear in mind that when we taper we reduce our energy expenditure, so if intake is similar we should be building up our stores as training reduces. Many make the mistake of gorging on bowls of pasta all week, but there are other factors to consider.

432. Think about it like fuelling a car. In your taper, if you're putting the same amount of petrol in, but driving the car less, then your tank will be nigh on full by the end of the week anyway. An extra top-up in the 24 to 48 hours before a race, without using any up, means you can get to the start line with a full tank.

433. Try not to carb-load in the 24 hours before your race starts, as this can cause gastrointestinal distress for some. Make sure the tank is already full with 24 hours to go, then just keep it topped up by reducing energy expenditure and eating light, carb-focused meals in the day before your race.

434. Try to avoid red meat the day before a race. It digests slowly and will either sit inside you for your race or come out at mile 10.

435. The advice around carb-loading suggests ingesting 5 to 10 grams of carbohydrate, per kilogram of body weight, in a day. So, if you weigh 70 kilograms, you're looking at 350 to 700 grams of carbohydrate. This is a big range, and it can be very individual, so test this out.

436. Female athletes need to consider that they could be burning different energy sources at an increased rate at different stages of their menstrual cycles; their overall body weight will have a lower percentage of muscle than an equivalent male athlete. Female athletes may be able to utilise more body fat at a given intensity than a male athlete, so all these factors need to be considered.

437. It is good to mix your types of carbo-hydrate, with glucose transported to muscle glycogen stores and fructose to liver glycogen stores, so that you can build up both.

438. On the morning of your race make sure there is some fructose in your pre-race meal, as this is the store you will have depleted overnight.

439. Your pre-race meal is another very individual factor that needs to be tested thoroughly. Some can eat an hour before a race, others need to get up at 3.00 a.m. to have breakfast. A light, carbohydrate-based meal, such as porridge with banana or jam, some toast with orange juice or even just a liquid breakfast, might be right for you, so try them out on your long run days.

440. Hydration levels are another individ-ual factor and with this come considerations for electrolytes too. Some research suggests that one can pre-load with electrolytes too, so having an electrolyte drink on the day before and on the morning of your race can be helpful.

Top buffet-grazing skills in evidence on the South Downs Way 50.   © *Pete Aylward, RunPhoto*

441. Don't just guess your electrolyte levels if you want to take your running seriously. It varies due to genetic and environmental factors, so you might as well use a sweat test to figure out what your body is losing in terms of sodium, the main electrolyte in your sweat, so you can replace it at the right level in your fluids. Don't confuse salt and sodium levels when working out your electrolytes; some brands list salt, others sodium.

442. If you're not able to get a sweat test then look for levels of sodium on your clothes post run to gauge whether you're a salty sweater or not. Equally, allow a dog to run around your running group after a long run and you'll find out who has the highest sodium concentration from how much attention their legs get from the hound. This is obviously slightly less scientific, but still a valid method.

RACE FOOD (443–474)

443. When runners talk of 'hitting the wall' it's generally a depletion of their glycogen stores. It's a bit like trying to run your car on an empty tank – although we are able to use stored body fat as fuel, just at a much lower intensity.

444. If you do hit that wall, slow down and get some sugar in. The quicker it can be absorbed, the better; energy drinks, cola, jelly babies or energy gels are ideal. Get the energy in and try to keep it coming in too.

445. A much better plan is to try and avoid depleting this store in the first place. First, make sure you start your race with a decent amount of glycogen stored on your body, some extra in your pockets (or race belt), a plan for the full distance and hopefully some checkpoints to help you along the way.

446. Aitor Viribay and his team of researchers studied some elite male (note that the study only included male athletes) ultra-runners ingesting 120 grams of carbohydrates per hour for six hours during a mountain ultra-race. The runners didn't experience significant gastrointestinal issues and they had less evidence of muscle damage at the end of the race. But this is just showing the higher end of what's possible – before you start mainlining energy gels into your eyeball.

447. First things first – work out what you usually take on during a race. How many grams of carbohydrate (not calories, because glugging olive oil won't help you) do you take on per hour during your races?

448. Now think about your energy demands for the race. This is influenced by the time you're out on the course, the intensity you're working at and your training background. It's likely we'll all still end up with a negative energy balance for a marathon, but how do we stop this affecting performance?

449. Ask yourself, is my fuelling affecting my performance? Are you seeing a significant slowdown in the second half of each race that could be explained by a depletion of your energy stores? For the most of us the answer will be 'yes' and there are two solutions: go at a lower intensity, therefore utilising more stored body fats as fuel, or eat more carbohydrates. Or both.

450. Figuring out your optimum level needs experimentation. It varies due to gender, phase of the menstrual cycle, muscle mass, day-to-day diet and training. You can train your gut to utilise and process more carbohydrates over the course of a race by training with progressively over-loaded amounts in the weeks building up to an event.

451. Starting from scratch? Begin with 30 to 40 grams of carbohydrates per hour. That could be two energy gels, 50 grams of Haribo, some squares of jam sandwiches or a 330-millilitre can of fizzy pop.

452. Be aware of the sugar tax. Some of your favourite energy-filled, teeth-rotting, sugary drinks have been reduced to lower levels of carbohydrates, therefore potentially better for the general population, but less good for marathon fuelling.

453. If you're racing for less than two hours, you can get by on a good bit of muscle and liver glycogen and lower amounts of carbohydrates during your race, around 30 to 40 grams per hour.

454. The longer you go, the more added carbohydrates you need trickling in, ideally every 10 to 20 minutes, to keep your energy levels up. The higher your intensity, the greater the likelihood is you'll burn a higher percentage of your fuel from glycogen stores, as opposed to the slower, but more easily stored, fuel from body fat.

455. If you're running for over two hours then start thinking about increasing your per-hour rates. See what works in your long runs and build-up races, and test a bit more each time, instead of just going for the highest possible amount you can imagine.

456. When getting to higher amounts, or earlier if you're experiencing gut sensitivity with the added carbohydrates, start taking a portion of your carbs on board as fructose. This is referred to as using 'multiple-transportable carbohydrates'. If you're taking on larger amounts of carbs than your gut can handle, then help the body out and use some fructose. In the study mentioned in *tip 446*, the athletes were given a 2:1 ratio of dextrose to fructose; this is similar to the carbo-hydrate drinks with 80 grams of carbs in, such as Maurten or SiS Beta Fuel.

457. When making up your carbohydrate drinks, you can add 500 or 600 millilitres of water as advised, or dilute them more, as long as you test before race day. If you know it's a hot day and you'll be drinking more, then maybe dilute your sports drink a little to avoid overloading the gut (but also consider your electrolytes; see *tip 467*).

458. If you have a single 80-gram carbohydrate drink packet in a litre of fluid, you could be taking in 40 grams of carbs per hour just through your drink. Then add in a couple of biscuits, jelly babies or an energy gel and you're really hitting some serious numbers.

459. If you're taking on all your energy through fluids then remember your electrolyte balance (I know this is repeated, but that's because it's important) and have a plan B. Always have a plan B, but especially if all your fuelling eggs are in one basket. Also, don't have eggs as your plan B.

460. Start learning what amounts and concentrations of nutrients are in different foods. It helps to increase your knowledge around your own race nutrition and is also helpful in races with strange checkpoints or if you go off-plan and have to adapt on the fly. Having a rough idea of how much a food type contributes to your needed hourly intake will allow you to make better-informed decisions mid race.

461. It doesn't have to be all sweet foods either; there are plenty of savoury options, like salted potatoes, that you could have instead. Look at the density of carbs in the food in question, think about the amount of carbs per 100 grams (very important if you have to carry the food) and consider having a mix of different foods for if you start getting flavour fatigue in the latter stages of races.

The more unnatural the colour of a drink, the more energy it provides.*   © James Vincent

462. There is a great book called *Feed Zone Portables*, by Biju Thomas and Allen Lim, that has a whole bunch of recipes for trail and road snacks. I probably should stop recommending other books as you've come to this one for all your solutions – right?

463. If you are starting to crave savoury food, it can be your body telling you that you need extra sodium because your electrolyte balance is out. Your brain is clever like that – it will generally point you in the right direction, but will likely not fix the problem quickly enough on its own.

464. If you're running so fast, in a marathon or longer race, that you can't eat anything, then you're running too fast. Period. Don't go telling me 'well, that's my marathon pace'. If you can't fuel that pace for the length of a marathon then you're not going to get to the end as quickly as your legs suggest.

465. Blocks to fuelling can be physical, but also mental too. We're used to being in a lifestyle where we eat what we want and if we don't want something then we can just pop to a 24-hour supermarket and get something different. That mindset can work against you in a marathon or ultra and when people say 'I couldn't eat any more' they often really mean 'I didn't want to eat any more', which is different.

466. Put the same effort into eating as you do to driving your legs forward. When you're struggling to get to the next lamp post ahead, but using all your will to keep pushing, remember you could have avoided running out of energy by putting that same effort level into eating an energy gel that was a bit too sickly.

467. If you're vomiting everything back up or it's coming out the other end at a high velocity, then maybe you are at the point where you can't eat any more. I did, however, run from kilometre 70 to 246 of the Greek Spartathlon while vomiting every 15 to 20 minutes. Yes, it wasn't pretty, but I kept eating and then throwing up the food and drink, but some of that energy must have been sneaking in, because I was able to keep going. That instance was actually down to electrolyte imbalance, coupled with poor pacing in the heat, so a bit more knowledge and planning might have avoided it. Electrolyte needs are very individual, but what is important is to make sure you're getting the right amount in relation to the amount of fluid you're taking on too.

* Possibly not true.

A runner taking part in the Lakeland Trails in the Lake District. © Pete Aylward, RunPhoto

468. This very much applies to super-long events too. While doing LEJOG, both the record holders, Carla Molinaro and Dan Lawson, suffered from painful mouth ulcers, but they knew they had to keep eating if they wanted to keep moving forward. They painfully ate for days on end to achieve their goals – remember that when that next energy gel tastes a little sticky at kilometre 24 and you can't be bothered any more.

469. Race food doesn't have to be horrible. Eating what you like is a useful tool; for example, if there is a food that doesn't have the best carb-to-weight ratio, but you like it, then it's worth considering. There are so many food options available; arm yourself with the knowledge of what your body needs and find a way to get it in a way that works for you.

470. Even if a food isn't particularly carb-rich, like cherry tomatoes, but it refreshes your palate and means you're more likely to eat that next energy gel, then it can be a useful part of your race fuelling plan. If you do prefer some foods that aren't particularly carb-rich, try to couple them with something that is, like a square of milk chocolate or some banana.

471. Make a plan and test it out in your long runs. Find out what works for you, whether you can improve it through practice and variation of your fuelling, and then eat like your race depends on it. This doesn't mean gorge yourself from kilometre one, it means giving the same importance to fuelling as you do to buying fancy go-faster race shoes and smiling for the race photographers.

472. If you're running an ultra then don't be afraid to slow down at checkpoints, or just in general, if it allows better fuelling. Those few seconds you saved blasting through that checkpoint don't really count for much when you're lying on the side of the trail, begging the Norse gods to send down a lightning bolt with some carbs attached.

473. If Bill Rodgers can walk and sip his water when winning the Boston Marathon, then you can take the time to nicely pick up your checkpoint food instead of throwing your arm across the whole table and sending all the jelly beans into the air.

474. Last, but not least, if you're going a really long way, over multiple hours or days, then consider adding 15- to 20-gram bursts of protein into your schedule, just as you might in a normal day. It's not the optimum fuel for endurance, but if your body is looking for some protein, it is better that there is some available rather than your body chowing down on your muscles.

INJURY* (475–506)

475. It's the dreaded i-word, the word that no runner wants to hear. But with some studies suggesting nearly 80 per cent of runners pick up an injury in any one calendar year, the first thing to do is avoid panicking.

476. Not every pain or niggle is an injury, but it's worth listening to your body as much as you can. If something is hurting during or after a run, then make a note of it in your training log. It might just be a tweaked ankle or a tight calf after speedwork, but if it happens after every interval session or gets worse over time then a record of its progression will be useful.

477. Don't just dive straight into Dr Google and come back with the worst-case scenario. Runners with stubbed toes have been known to spend 15 minutes on the internet and self-diagnose a femoral stress fracture or RED-S. Most injuries aren't the worst-case scenario, and plenty don't even require you to stop running.

478. When it comes to getting advice around injuries, or any subject really, try to get it from people who know what they're talking about. Injury advice from someone who isn't a qualified practitioner could be great, but it could also be total rubbish. It's more likely to be from a very narrow window of experience – their own – rather than the wider learning and evidence-based experience of a qualified expert.

479. To start, it's best to think about things that might help you avoid an injury. A 'pre-hab' routine targeted towards individual weaknesses and imbalances could prove important in preventing injuries in the first place. If you can, it is worth seeing a physiotherapist on a semi-regular basis, once a month or bi-monthly, to help identify your strengths and weaknesses.

480. I've not taken a back hander to help line the pockets of physios worldwide – put your tinfoil hat away. Like coaching, to get the best out of your physio, it is important to get to know each other and for the physio to get to know your body.

481. It's not just because I'm extremely loyal but, even if I seek a second opinion elsewhere, I'll always check in with Sarah, my physio, about a potential diagnosis from another physio. A good physio just wants to see you pain-free and running well.

482. Over time a physio will learn more about what works for you, and can also help prevent you from getting injured in the first place by noticing potential issues and helping you work on imbalances and niggles before they stop you running.

* Thank you to Sarah Tunstall, my physiotherapist and GB mountain runner, for her help with this section.

THE RUNNER'S BODY (403–554)

483. If the injury is bad enough that you can't run or it just keeps getting worse, then speak to a physiotherapist. One benefit of the COVID-19 pandemic was more experts making themselves readily available for consultations online at affordable rates. Take advantage of this.

484. The first thing I always think about when I get injured is how has this happened? You might think that most running injuries happen when running, but it could just as easily be a slip on a wet floor at work or lifting a box badly. The more information you have, the better.

485. Does running make this worse? If I can go out for a run and there are no ill effects to the injury, then I might stick to some easy running. The second anything makes it feel worse, I'll stop and rest. Sometimes soft tissue injuries can respond well to movement and stopping running completely can sometimes cause additional stiffness and deconditioning of muscles. If this is the case, often pain will subside as you run and it may be possible to keep running at a reduced pace, on flatter surfaces or for a shorter duration or frequency.

486. As a general rule, if pain persists throughout a run, or gets worse, it is important to rest and seek advice. Also, if pain is worse the following day, this is another sign that a break from running should be considered.

487. If you are unsure about a niggle, then it's worth making your running route several smaller loops near home, or running on a treadmill. You don't want to do a Super Hans and get 30 kilometres away from home and realise that you can't get back. Or worse, you can get back, but it'll make your injury worse.

488. If you are given exercises to do by your physio, make sure that you do them. Physiotherapy is never a magic bullet and is a dual effort between client and practitioner. If you work hard to address underlying strength deficits, physiotherapy treatment will be much more effective.

489. When your injury starts to improve, keep in contact with your physio and don't just stop doing your exercises. Go in for a visit when you're injury-free so they can advise on next steps to prevent the same thing happening again.

490. Runners are not known for their patience but a good philosophy to adopt is, if you start to feel better, wait at least one more day before going for a run.

491. Pain is not 'weakness leaving the body'. Pain is your body's signal that it doesn't like something and isn't to be confused with hard work and muscular fatigue during workouts. If you're experiencing pain during or after your run, don't ignore it.

492. Give your physio time to help you solve any problems before jumping ship to a different one. It's a partnership and you need to work together. Communication and understanding between both parties usually lead to the best results. Sarah wanted me to remind runners that physios are never right 100 per cent of the time, and runners are often very in tune with their bodies, so listening to each often leads to longer-term solutions.

493. If it really isn't working with a physiotherapist then a good one will recommend another physio, or might recommend a different kind of specialist to see. Every physiotherapist undergoes different training, has different experience and employs different techniques, so it is important to find what and who works for you. If you spend 12 months with them simply massaging the same spot and nothing is happening to your injury, then maybe, just maybe, you're just paying their Wi-Fi bill.

494. There are other types of people to go and visit when injured (or just for pre-hab), such as osteopaths, chiropractors, acupuncturists, sports therapists or massage therapists. You might discover someone who helps you stay injury-free and that's what counts. Try to think objectively about what's going on and be wary of giving your money to someone who has made up their own speciality.

495. Get yourself some resistance bands. They're not expensive and it will really increase the range of exercises you can do at home.

496. Running rarely involves linear, symmetrical movements and we are regularly required to turn corners, jump dog leads or negotiate mud and hills, so being strong in different directions is vital. Small resistance bands are great because different angles and more specific movements can be strengthened, unlike on some gym equipment. They are also great for any trips away as they take up no space at all. It's easier than trying to find a gym near your hotel or your friend's house.

497. Keep an eye on motivation levels when injured too, as it can be easy to let your head dip and then everything feels even tougher.

498. When off injured, it might be worth paying some attention to your nutrition. If you're normalised to taking in the right amount for your higher activity levels and suddenly you've greatly reduced output, then it could create a surplus.

499. This doesn't mean you should starve yourself when injured – far from it – your body will need the nutrients and fuel to repair too. It's just worth paying attention to your diet and it's not necessary to be right on your racing weight when out injured. It might also be a factor that has led to your injury.

500. Your injury might allow you to focus on other aspects of your training, such as strength and conditioning or mobility work, or repairing any kit that needs some love, planning your next races or doing some non-running activities that you might have neglected a bit recently.

501. Focus on your progress rather than comparison with your last race. It can be disheartening if you're 'just' back to running 5K pain-free and it's quite slow, but that could be an almighty step in the right direction and a really positive moment.

502. Set yourself small goals and targets along the way. Having to build back up to where you were pre-injury might take some time, so having a few benchmarks en route will keep that smile on your face and remind you that you're still trucking along nicely.

503. Planning a race can be a good motivator for your come-back, but don't let it weigh too heavily on your mind or think you have to prove yourself. Everybody heals at different rates and only you know what you've had to endure, so don't let other people's expectations impact your early performances after injury. If the day comes and you're not ready, don't be afraid to skip it. It's better to focus on your development than rush and cause a backward step.

504. If you're thinking of skipping the race because you won't run a PB, then try to focus on just doing the best you can on the day. It's your post-injury PB and a mark to improve on in the future. We don't have to run a PB in every race and sometimes it's good to just measure where you are and enjoy the thrill of the chase.

THE RUNNER'S BODY (403-554)

505. When you get back to training with your friends, be wary of trying to replicate where you were before. Your rate of perceived exertion is affected not just by the physical factors but where you think you should be with respect to your mates. If you feel like your mate Dawn should be behind you, but she's not had an injury and has been training well, it's going to feel harder mentally to keep up with her too. There will be a bit of ego at play too, but just try to relax and run at a pace that's right for you and your recovery.

506. Build back up gradually, as doing too much too soon can set you back. It's not quite the 10 per cent every week idea, as you're likely building back up to your own previous levels reasonably quickly, but respect the easy volume, as increasing volume and high-stress workouts too quickly post-injury is asking for trouble.

FEET (507-521)

507. Feet are the main point of contact between you and the ground you run on (unless you fall, then it's your face). These five-toed wonders attached to our ankles deserve looking after and, if they're in pain, it'll change the way you run and lower your chances of getting a PB or even a finish.

508. When choosing shoes *(tips 720–728)* keep comfort in mind. Lightweight is great, but if you can't even think about putting your foot down without wincing a little, then the performance gain of lightweight shoes goes out the window.

509. Before you think about the shoes, get yourself some good socks. It's an area many will scrimp on, but it's a false economy. Cheap socks fall apart quicker, smell worse and can even help cause blisters and sweating.

510. What socks you need can change from season to season and race to race; come race day I prefer a tight-fitting pair that are breathable and not too thick. How a sock interacts with a shoe can affect your feet too and a pairing of shoes and socks, which both work fantastically on their own, may cause blisters on a hot day.

511. Run-specific socks are a worthwhile investment, especially if they have the little L and R to tell you which foot to put them on. I'm not sure if the socks are different at all, but it'll make you feel like a pro.

512. Normally before a race I'll apply a layer of Vaseline®, or a different lubricant, such as Squirrel's Nut Butter, to my feet so they don't rub. Be careful to clean your feet beforehand – don't slather your mucky feet with lubricant so the little bits of grit or dirt get stuck.

513. When you feel a blister coming on, a hot spot, you've got two options. Stop and sort it or carry on and deal with it after the race. The length of race and how close to the finish you are may impact this decision.

514. A blister can also change the way you run so consider where the blister is and how much of an impact it could have if it gets worse and what this might mean up the chain. In a long race a simple blister untreated can become a knee, quad or hip issue because you're running funny.

515. If you're on a training run, then stop and try to sort out a blister. It might only look like a little red spot when you take your shoe off, but within a kilometre or two that can be raw skin and it's going to affect your training for the days to come too.

Look after your feet and if you need to take off your shoes to do so, take the time. Trash your feet and you'll trash your times.   © *James Vincent*

516. Initially look for what is irritating the foot. It could be some dirt or sand, a kink in the lining of the shoe or … I don't know … a gold star your kid superglued on to your sock? Then get rid of it if you can.

517. If the blister has already formed, you have a few options. The first is to just ignore it until you finish, which may become quite painful, especially if it bursts. If you take the shoe off to inspect then even putting it back on again could be difficult.

518. The second is to drain the blister yourself, but remember it's protecting the irritated skin underneath from further rubbing and infection. Ideally you use a sterile needle or syringe to take the fluid out, clean the area and apply a sterile bandage to your foot.

519. If you do drain your blister then try to make the hole small, a few small holes might be better than one, rather than just gashing it open, as this lowers the risk of infection. Unless you make this small hole with a rusty fork, which increases the risk somewhat.

520. When your race is over, take good care of your blister. If it's not burst and you can put on shoes or sandals that allow it to stay intact, then it's best to keep it that way. It allows your skin to heal while still protected.

521. If it has burst, then make sure you clean it well with antiseptic and dry it afterwards. A bandage will keep the area clean while it heals; the risk of infection is your biggest issue, so this is a good idea. If you have to take a few days off to allow healing, then so be it, because an infection will cause a longer lay-off.

MENSTRUAL CYCLE* (522-537)

522. Right: periods and the menstrual cycle. They affect 50 per cent of our running community and most shy away from the discussion. Chaps: don't even think about skipping this section, you might learn something.

523. For female runners, you might have to deal with being on your period for a race. The chances are the organisation hasn't really taken this into account and you'll need to plan ahead for different scenarios, especially if you're due on, haven't already started and it's a long race.

524. If race organisers have planned entirely from a male-centric point of view with their facilities, it's worth letting them know about it as I hope they want to improve for the future.

525. Check out checkpoint facilities and even ask the race directors if it's not clear, so you at least know of a few hygienic spots along the trail that are there if you need them. Worst case scenario: carry hand sanitiser and tissues and use the bins.

526. Ultra-racing still has a long way to go in terms of gender equality, especially as the races get longer. On the plus side, it might mean that at the start there is a 50/50 split of toilets and only 10 per cent of the field are women, so that's a win at least.

527. Some female runners have had success using menstrual cups as they can hold a larger volume before needing to be replaced, but as with anything, try practising and testing out different kit on your long runs. This can include trying out different products to help you race while on your period.

528. There are companies trying to address the lack of focus for women training through their period and one example is Iceni Silver sportswear. Started by two British mums who felt they too often heard of their daughters and their friends skipping sport or fearing the start of their period, it's good to see products specifically for sporty women out there.

529. Talk to other female runners that you know and try to see if they can help, as open communication might reveal very similar problems that others are facing too, but some will have great solutions you haven't thought of.

530. If you're a coach of female athletes, then learning about the menstrual cycle is an important part of your job. Sharing with your athletes that you are trying to learn more can also be an effective way of opening up important conversations that will help you both plan training and racing in the future.

531. As an athlete, try to be open with your coach, but they should understand it's a two-way street and many people are not comfortable discussing what is essentially a big factor in female athletes' health and training. Hopefully this will continue to change and great resources like the *Female Athlete Podcast* should be required listening for everyone in our sport.

532. I'd love to say we're at a stage where athletes can plan their training around their menstrual cycle, but levels of understanding and research are still developing. One of the most important things to do is track your own cycle and symptoms in your training log.

533. How you train and feel at different stages of your cycle can be very individual. Some athletes feel stronger at the start, others are exhausted at that time. Regularly noting your own reactions to certain types of training, and tracking your period, can provide a case study of one for you and your coach to learn from.

* Thank you to Sophie Grant, ultra-runner and fellow coach, for her help with this section.

534. To track your periods, there are apps, such as FitrWoman, or you can use an online spreadsheet, or add an additional column to programmes such as Training-Peaks; the main thing is to find something that you are comfortable using.

535. A normal menstrual cycle can be anything from 21 to 35 days; it can be a useful indicator of good health. If you're experiencing amenorrhea (missed periods) or irregular periods, this can be a sign of low energy availability and further issues.

536. Your nutritional demands can change around your period too; at different stages of your cycle, you might have a higher demand for fats or carbohydrates. It can also affect your ability to undertake different types of session, but can still be very individual, so taking note of your own cycle and symptoms is still the best plan of action.

537. We all need to talk about the menstrual cycle more openly. It's a huge part of the training equation for 50 per cent of runners and just because it doesn't affect you doesn't mean you shouldn't and couldn't help. And no, Creepy Dave, that doesn't mean you can go to the running club and start asking everyone about their period. Start by educating yourself.

SLEEP DEPRIVATION (538–554)

538. If you are running through the night in a race or going for a fastest known time, then chances are you've thought about sleep deprivation. Running through the world when everyone else is asleep is pretty special and you should try it at least once. When the sun starts to creep over the horizon it can really feel powerful.

539. The two factors to take into account are your circadian rhythm and the build-up of adenosine in your brain. These two things will put you to sleep on the trail.

540. Firstly, the circadian rhythm makes you sleepy at the right times. Mela-tonin in the body makes you tired when the sun goes down and then you are used to your normal time frame for getting up. If you are running overnight then expect this to play a part.

541. If you're running overseas then your circadian rhythm can also be affected by jet lag. It might be the middle of the day where you are, but if your body thinks it's 3.00 a.m. then you're going to feel it.

542. You can try to avoid this by staying up until your normal bedtime when you reach a new time zone. If you go to sleep at your normal time then you're likely to adapt a little more slowly; but power through to your new bedtime, wake up fresh in the morning and the effects can be lessened.

543. Secondly, adenosine builds up when you miss sleep and the only thing that really dissipates it is actual sleep.

544. Caffeine, that wonderful friends of ours, will block the adenosine receptors, so your brain is less affected by the increasing amounts of adenosine, but it does not get rid of it. So, if you do use caffeine, in whatever form, know that it's merely stemming the tide, and the waves of sleepiness will grow ever stronger until you have a proper kip.

545. Shorter sleeps of less than 30 minutes are sometimes referred to as a 'power nap'; anything longer than that and you'll enter deeper stages of sleep. Getting woken up in the middle of one of the deeper stages of sleep can actually make you feel worse.

Trail running in the Brecon Beacons, Wales. © John Coefield

546. A power nap can work as a quick release valve, but to really clear your head you need to have a full 90-minute sleep cycle (or three). Each consecutive sleep cycle is deeper and more effective than the last.

547. Some runners will only take very small sleeps, from as little as two to ten minutes, in an attempt to trick their brain into allowing some more hours of running and hopefully get through to sunrise or to the next checkpoint for a proper sleep.

548. Build-up of adenosine increases when you're not taking on sufficient fuel to support your activities, so eating enough and going slower can potentially reduce its impact on your night of running.

549. When you are sleep-deprived you make poorer decisions in general, from what to eat and where to go to whether or not you should just stop for a sleep. And you faff about and waste a lot of time too. If you are pushing through the night, think about the value of it. A well-rested runner will move a lot quicker the next day and a 90-minute or three-hour sleep can quickly be recouped on faster legs.

550. If you are power napping in the wilds, then think about where you do this. If the chances are you'll wake up cold, then sleeping at the foot of a climb is much more sensible than sleeping at the top. A descent will only chill you more, whereas a hefty climb will have you toasty by the top.

551. With any 20- to 30-minute power nap, it's worth taking on some fuel and caffeine beforehand, as the caffeine takes about 20 minutes to kick in. That way you'll wake up ready to take on the world, or just chatting a lot more rubbish than usual. Either way it'll help keep you awake for the next few hours.

552. On multi-day trips longer than 72 hours, it's not really worth skimping on sleep completely, as the chances are you'll lose any time saved as you'll be so sleep-deprived.

553. If you want to push the limits of sleep deprivation in a race, then make sure you're on top of everything else, like your navigation, fuelling and pacing. If you are lacking in one of these fundamental areas, then an implosion is more likely.

554. If you're planning on a tiny sleep then sometimes it helps to not be too comfortable. On his LEJOG run, Dan Lawson chose to sleep for two minutes on the side of the A9, rather than in the lovely camper van we had, as he figured it would be harder to get out of the van post-nap. He also felt the same about pooing, which probably didn't save as much time when you account for the time he spent climbing into fields and bushes and so on.

The serious trail runner always makes sure their kit matches. Paul Radford always matches.   © Robbie Britton

Classic conditions on the Ben Nevis Ultra.   © Pete Aylward, RunPhoto

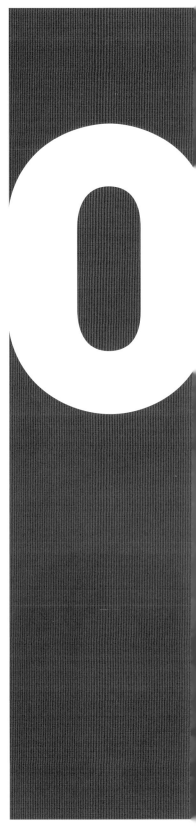

006

RACING (555-719)

'No matter how much you swear you'll never do it again, you will sign up for another race. Normally within a matter of days. Sometimes hours.'

RACING (555-719)

THE PRE-RACE TOILET
(555–563)

555. Before you get to the start line of any race think about your drills. I don't mean your running drills, but your toilet drills. Do you need one, two or three visits to the Portaloo before the gun goes?

556. Check the queues out and if you see a short queue, it's often worth jumping in, just in case you need a wee or a quick poo by the time you get to the front of the queue. You'll just be standing around listening to Bob from the club talk about how great his training has been going otherwise.

557. Take your own toilet paper. You can guarantee by the time you get to the front someone will come out and apologise for using the last bit. Be prepared.

558. For the love of God, wash your hands after visiting those cesspits. Runners, for whatever reason, are not great at using toilets; maybe they're just more feral than most from pooing in bushes too often. Make sure that you wash your hands and use some antibacterial gel if you can. Over the course of the next 30 minutes to however many hours of racing, you're going to touch your face a million times. Best not have your hands covered in someone else's faecal matter from the start. Or your own.

559. Trust the queue. If the start time is getting close and you still need to go, wait it out. The line will move quicker as others bottle it and head to the start, and it's probably better to start a few seconds late, rather than have to stop a few miles down the road in someone's daffodils.

560. If you're having regular, real issues with your stomach before a race then start to note and reflect on your pre-race diet and maybe consider if it's pre-race anxiety too.

561. Some will do a short warm-up run, way before the start of their race, not to warm up the leg muscles, but the sphincter. Even five or ten minutes may be enough to shake out that wee demon that you don't want to carry with you for a marathon.

562. If, by this tip, you're somewhat uncomfortable talking so much about poo, maybe reconsider that step up to ultra-running.

563. If you're unsure about your stomach, then take a little bit of loo roll with you in a plastic bag *(tips 947–948)*. It weighs nothing and saves you having to use a sock. Don't scrimp on how much you carry too, as four sheets might not be enough and eight could be a race saver.

ON THE START LINE (564–572)

564. Don't try anything new on race day. It's an old tip, but it bears repeating. It can be tempting, as many new foods, drinks and equipment might be available to try at the race expo the day before, but save it for after the race.

565. Before you put your race number on, scrunch it up into a little ball and then flatten it out again. Then when you pin the number on it's more likely to fit closer to your top and won't flap around in the wind as much.

566. If you want some extra cheers during the race, wear something with your name on. If you want some laughs, wear something with someone else's name on. No one else will get the joke but it might make you smile at some of the toughest moments.

We're not sure what's going on in the bottom left of this picture, we'll let you caption this one yourselves. © Tim Lloyd

567. If you're a sweaty runner like I am then have a think about having an old-school sweat band or Buff® around your wrist, just to help keep all the salt out of your eyes.

568. On the start line, smile and wish the other runners good luck. It's a nice thing to do, but it'll also help you relax and maybe you'll even psych some of them out by being too friendly if it's a road race. The Italians say '*in bocca al lupo*', which translates as 'into the wolf's mouth', but is just a much cooler way of saying 'good luck'.

569. Make sure your laces are tied nicely before the gun goes off. Not so tight to mean that you can't feel your feet by halfway round, but a loose lace at kilometre 25 of a marathon is going to annoy you more than anything else (although some will welcome the distraction).

570. For those with longer hair, make sure it's secure and isn't going to go all over the place on the way round. It might look good to have the wind blowing through your locks, but when you want to shove an energy gel down your throat you don't want to accidentally feed it into your hair.

571. Get your GPS watch ready a few minutes before the start. No one is going to wait if you don't have your satellites yet.

572. Prepare yourself, take some deep breaths and remember this is the fun part. It's what all the hard work is about, so try to enjoy yourself, at least until it gets really tough (which is down to how you pace, I guess).

THE GUN GOES OFF (573–589)

573. Remember that adrenaline is going to try to let you get carried away for that first kilometre, but then leave you to pay off the bills in the second half of your race. Don't leave it all out there in kilometre one, unless there's a bottleneck coming up. Then just go crazy and deal with the consequences later.

574. Don't get too worried about being a bit behind your goal pace in kilometre one either. If it's crowded there might be some stopping and starting, juking around runners who've overestimated their starting pace (chaps, I'm looking at you) and generally just a bit of time to get into your rhythm.

Passing the Ribblehead Viaduct on the Three Peaks Race in the Yorkshire Dales. Think it must have been a muddy one. © Pete Aylward, RunPhoto

RACING (555-719)

575. If you find yourself at the front, make sure you concentrate on where you're going, or everyone will follow you when you go the wrong way.

576. If you're not first, then don't just blindly follow the people ahead. They might be going the wrong way and you could then nip into first place.

577. Use your watch and heart rate on race day, but don't be governed by the stats. They can be a useful guide in the early kilometres to avoid starting too fast or holding your pace in some faster kilometres in the middle, but when the going gets tough, focus on you.

578. If you're well into the second half of your race and your watch is telling you to slow down, it's probably best to ignore it. The second half of a race is far too late to be sensible (unless you're running 200 kilometres, then you've probably got time for a cup of tea and a rethink).

579. Don't leave it too late to start eating. Some people think that you should let the 80 to 90 minutes worth of glycogen you've stored in your carb-loading deplete, and then start eating, but by then it's too late.

580. Start eating early, but practise this in training too, as you might struggle a little further on into the event. If you know that by kilometre 25 you're in dire straits, make sure you stick to your plan and eat when it tells you to.

581. If you have one type of food, be it energy gels, flapjacks or sweets, that you're getting sick of, then try and eat one more lot before moving on to the alternatives. Unless you only have that food and no plan B or C. Then just keep the fuel going in with the same focus and determination you use to keep running forward.

582. When packing your food in race belts, vest, pockets, stuffed into your bra or taped to your wrist, think about how easy it will be to access and if you can make it any easier. If that back pocket is a swine to open when running at marathon pace then when the going gets tough, you're less likely to eat the energy gels stored there.

583. If you do have difficult pockets, then eat that food first. You're still feeling good, happy to faff around with a stupidly placed pocket and less likely to drop the energy gel on the floor when it's out.

584. Take note if any of your food is harder to eat with a dry mouth, like bits of flapjack, as you're less likely to chow down on that in the second half of a race.

585. Every kilometre or so think about your form. Eyes up; looking up the road not on the floor; drive your arms back; run smoothly. Having a list or mantra can help you stay focused on the task at hand. I've previously used the chorus of Ben Howard's 'Keep Your Head Up' as a mantra with both physical and physiological cues during a race. It's unclear whether Ben is an ultra-runner but I'm sure that is what the song was intended for.

586. When planning food to eat during a race, base your schedule on time, not distance. Even on a 'flat' road marathon not all kilometres are created equal; 5K in the first half might be flatter (and therefore quicker) than an undulating 5K in the second half. If you're eating every 5K then you'll have a bigger gap in your plan when you need the energy most. And this is suggesting you'll pace evenly, which most won't.

587. If you do have to eat regularly and you know you're not good at it, then you can set a timer on your watch to beep at you every 20 or 30 minutes and you know you have to chow down.

588. If you do check your watch too often, then try setting a screen only with information you need, such as time for eating and heart rate, instead of always seeing your current pace, which can give erroneous readings, especially in cities with high-rise buildings.

589. Still want to record your run, but find that nothing good at all comes from looking at your watch? A piece of electrical tape across the screen will solve that problem. Cheaper than breaking the screen before each race too.

WHEN THE GOING GETS TOUGH (590-595)

590. First, analyse why it's got tough. Did you start too fast, not eat enough or has a time goal just gone out of reach. Some are easier to solve than others, depending on the race distance.

591. If your problem isn't solvable in the time you have left, i.e. you started too fast and you're six kilometres from the end of the race, then skip to the tips about techniques for coping emotionally on race day *(tips 596–620)*. You're in for a rough ride, so let's make the best of it and get you through to the end. If you're reading this at kilometre 35 of a marathon and trying to figure out a plan, then drop the book, it's well heavy.

592. The problem-solving skills necessary here vary according to the distance of race you're in. For a 5K or 10K there is often very little time to correct anything, so using psychological skills to get to the end, but learning for next time, might be your best bet. Allowing yourself to ease back for a couple of minutes might help, but by then you're nearly at the finish anyway.

593. Getting up to half marathon and beyond, even one energy gel or an eased back kilometre can make a difference. If you've hit the wall then it can be a race saver to have that quick energy hit in there and even just the carbs hitting your tongue has been shown to improve performance.

594. The research of Asker Jeukendrup, amongst others, has shown that if a simple carb drink is swished around the mouth (rather than swallowed) during exercise, an improvement in performance (similar to that which would have been gained if the drink were swallowed) is observed. This is potentially more useful in shorter races; in most longer races you might as well swallow the drink, as you'll probably need it later anyway.

595. If it's a hot spot or even a dreaded blister that's causing your problem *(tips 513–519)*, then once again the distance to the finish line affects how you can deal with it. The closer the finish line is, the more likely it is that you just need to embrace the pain and keep going. It might even be a welcome distraction from the pain in your legs from going too fast down that hill. A popped blister also poses an infection risk, so keep that in mind when dealing with them mid race or in a wilderness situation. At the very least, give it a good clean when you've finished racing or have got back to civilisation.

A RACING MIND (596–620)

596. A lot of the time training and racing advice is solely focused on the physiological aspects of endurance; however, psychological factors are not only equally important, but they're also all intertwined. The body and the mind don't work in isolation and the term 'psychobiological' is being seen more in training research.

597. The mind is a power tool, but it can negatively affect your running as well. It may well have the focus of living a long and healthy life, free from pain and danger, in-built. We're hard-wired to survive, and sometimes an all-out sprint at the end of a 5K goes against that innate desire to live past the next meal. Running 10,000 years ago, when you might have had to escape a predator at any moment, meant the brain benefited from keeping a little in reserve.

598. Focus forwards, rather than backwards, especially when it gets harder. Beyond the simple fact that twisting your neck to look behind you is mechanically inefficient for someone trying to go forward, it forces you into a negative thought process of 'they're catching me; I'm doing really badly'.

599. If people are overtaking you, just look straight ahead and focus on one runner you're gaining on. One runner is all it takes to find a positive: work on reeling that one runner in, rather than the thousands streaming past you.

600. Take a look at Samuele Marcora's research on perception of effort. It's brilliant. Simply, how we perceive our situation can have a huge impact on how we react to it.

601. For example, two clones (a bit sci-fi, I know) are in identical races, with identical environmental conditions, training, magic shoes and so on. At 30 kilometres both have run the same pace, eaten the same things and everything else is identical. But Runner A is being overtaken by everyone around them and Runner B is overtaking everyone nearby. The physiological situation is identical. The body is experiencing the same stresses in both scenarios, but think about how each individual runner is going to feel? Runner B will be flying, whereas Runner A will feel like they are running through treacle.

602. Think about how we can use this to our own advantage. As above, if we focus on the one runner who's paced it worse than we have (if this is the case we really need to talk about your pacing), then it can potentially impact how we perceive our own effort.

603. The flip side is that if we pace sensibly and fuel well, not only will we be physically in a better place, but mentally our perception of effort will be lower too, as we cruise pass those first-half heroes.

604. Next comes self-talk, a tried and tested mental skills technique for getting the most out of ourselves. Ideally it comes from someone else, shouting at you from the sidelines, and following you through those toughest kilometres, but it still works if we're shouting (externally or internally) at ourselves.

605. If you are talking to yourself in a race, then do it as an imaginary coach on your shoulder: 'you can do this'; 'you can dig deeper'; or 'keep going, Winston'. Research has shown this is more effective than: 'I can do this'; 'I can dig deeper'; or 'I can keep going'. It's best to stop this after the finish line though, especially by the time you're on social media, unless you're the Hulk, then you can do what you want. 'HULK SMASH PB.'

606. When it gets tough, break down the task into manageable chunks and deal with them one at a time. This advice works for both racing and life.

607. The harder a task gets, the smaller a chunk needs to be, but don't break it down into individual steps too early. Take the marathon. Start out just clocking off five kilometres at a time; avoid looking at that watch and try to focus on your rhythm, effort level and fuelling. When five kilometres feels like a long way, just make it through the next five kilometres and then think 'right, now to the next checkpoint', which might be two kilometres away.

608. As the going gets tougher, go a kilometre or a mile at a time, depending on how metric you're feeling. If you're feeling fancy then go a mile at a time first, and then swap to a kilometre at a time. The mental arithmetic might distract from the leg pain; however, think about mental fatigue too.

609. When a kilometre feels like a long way, pick a target in the distance, be it a slowing runner, a big tree or a bridge you can see. The further away, the better at first. Just focus your energy on getting there. Convince your brain that is all it has to do … for now. Then when you get there, pick another target ahead. Joke with your brain 'oh sorry, I meant that next bridge, you can do this'.

610. Then it might just be a sign 100 metres ahead, a bench 50 metres ahead or the next five steps. Find something that still feels manageable and get there, then renegotiate with yourself. Break it down into smaller, manageable chunks and, before you know it, the finish line will be in sight. It always gets physically closer if you work for it, unless it's a 24-hour race.

611. Marathon legend Paula Radcliffe took it to another level again, counting steps to while away the hard kilometres. This focuses the mind on the task at hand at the simplest level. It distracts from the time itself, might help an athlete keep up a good rhythm and if it worked for Paula running 2:15, then it must be good.

612. In both training and racing we can use positive mental imagery and visualisation off to help us achieve our goals. In training (or even as you drift off to sleep at night) you can visualise your race going well, running strong in the final kilometres and bursting through the finish line for a big PB. It is a way of rehearsing mentally for the big day, allowing your mind and body to prepare physically for that moment in the future, as well as boosting confidence.

613. Another way to use visualisation is with negative imagery. Go through the process of your worst-case scenarios and play out how you will react to these. Dropping your drink mid race? What will you do? Falling over at the start? Go through the thought process of getting up and continuing strong. Go through your 'what ifs … '.

614. With negative visualisation, try to limit its use close to races, as it can, for some, impact confidence and alter a positive mindset. Use it for troubleshooting an event way beforehand, build up your plan B and C, construct a plan to avoid needing to go to plan B and then have them stored and ready to use, if necessary.

615. Mindfulness is very much in fashion these days. There is even a whole bundle of apps to try out and runners have particularly found this useful in the taper phase of training, when the mind is prone to go wild with theories of injury and disaster (tips 241–242).

616. Mindfulness means connecting with the moment – the act of running in the present, rather than being distracted by other noises around. It's essentially a form of meditation for those who like moving their feet fast and many of us might already do this, but it's becoming more difficult with all the added 'noise' of running tech. The benefits can be that we focus on what matters – our breathing, our form, our fuelling – and can dampen out what doesn't matter.

617. On the other hand, mind wandering, psychologically speaking, is the opposite. Letting the mind wander and disassociate with the task in the present potentially means that we can disassociate from the pain or discomfort of a race or training effort.

618. Mind wandering can be both positive and negative though. While it might be excellent to allow the mind to troubleshoot other areas of life during a long run, if you're trying to master the skill of running downhill, then you really want the mind along for the ride, as that skill isn't just physical or neuromuscular.

619. All of these mental skills can be practised and improved. That's why we call them skills. Go out and use your long runs to practise mind wandering or mindfulness – you choose – and then use your threshold runs or intervals to work on talking to yourself and positive imagery.

620. Much has been written on the psychological aspect of running; *Endurance Performance in Sport*, edited by Carla Meijen, and *Performing Under Pressure*, by Josephine Perry, are both great. For wider training and life, *Mindset*, by Carol Dweck, and *Endure*, by Alex Hutchinson, provide some interesting insight.

Run your own race, even if that means you leave everyone behind. © Tim Lloyd

RACING (555-719)

MULTI-DAY RACING (621-653)

621. Multi-day races, such as the Marathon des Sables or the Beyond the Ultimate race series, are an enjoyable and challenging format. They are popular, but can be pretty expensive, even before you start buying kit.

622. Any race that calls itself 'the toughest race on earth' isn't. Just in case you were wondering.

623. Although traditional multi-day races can be up to 250 kilometres over five to seven days, they're generally not as tough as a one-off 150-kilometre race, even though you have to carry your kit for the week and the longest day can be 80 kilometres on its own.

624. Any well-trained and well-prepared endurance athlete can enjoy a multi-day race. Ideally, you'll be comfortable with the distance covered on the longest day beforehand, but there are as many logistical challenges as physical ones.

625. When training for such an endeavour, it's tempting to just try and replicate the race in your training with long days, backpack carrying and going up and down sand dunes, but it's not that simple.

626. Your fitness is one aspect, but you can train with the longest day in mind and add in some additional elements to cover the multi-day race format.

627. Practise running while carrying your pack, but not every day. Each session you do has a purpose; carrying a loaded pack might prevent you from getting the best of what you actually wanted from that run.

628. A few months out, start doing your long runs while carrying a pack – take some practice race food and a full load of water, as even that will be a couple of kilograms and will provide a good start to getting used to carrying gear. As you get closer to your race, start increasing the load on your longer runs, but again, not all of them. If you have higher-intensity sections within that long run, then think about whether a fully loaded pack will help or hinder the goal of that session.

629. Early doors, it's worth starting to think about specifically which pack you will be using in the race. To do that, you need to think about your kit list and race food too, as it all needs to go in there.

630. If you already have a 15- to 20-litre backpack that you're comfortable in then, it could be an easy decision. A new pack isn't always better, especially if yours is comfortable and you're used to it. A couple of repairs or improvements you could do yourself might make the pack perfect for the desert, jungle or frozen tundra.

631. As well as adequate storage and comfort, a key factor is accessibility. You need pockets and the like on your front. If you have to store your food in the back, then chances are you won't eat it when you need to. This goes for all ultras, but especially multi-day ultras.

632. Adding an extra set of pockets and storage around your waist can be a good way of keeping food and essentials in reach. Plenty of brands make waist belts; I'm a fan of the Naked® Running Band. They can be a little constrictive if rammed too full, but they add some great options to your set-up.

Running in your club vest is something special; here's my North Norfolk Beach Runners beauty. © *Zoe Salt*

633. Pack your bag with the items you're least likely to need at the bottom, but also take weight into account as too much weight high up in your pack can cause back issues. Keep anything you think you're going to need access to during the day in front pockets or at the top of the main section.

634. Test the pack and look for chafing when it's loaded too. If it rubs on a long run on your local trails with a sack of chickpeas inside, then it'll tear a full layer of skin off in your race. No one likes to lose a layer of skin during a race.

635. Talking of layers of skin going missing: that's a good segue to your feet. While having horrifically grim pictures to scare your mates afterwards might be a silver lining, poor foot care can make your race a horrible experience. See *tips 507–521* on foot care and blisters. For a multi-day race, you also need to consider how you can look after your trotters in between days too.

636. An extra pair of socks might not seem like a luxury item at first (then you'll be weighing your pack and replacing them with an extra pack of sweets of equal weight); consider taking both. Fresh socks, especially if you can wash the old pair and have them fresh-ish for the next day, can make the world of difference. Almost like new feet.

637. Air your feet in the evenings if you can, but only after giving them a good clean and dry. This does depend on conditions, as doing this in the Arctic could induce frostbite.

638. Grit and dirt can get into your shoes and ruin your race, but sand is especially adept at sneaking in through every little crevice. You can buy different styles of ready-made gaiters; some runners have silk ones custom made and sewed directly on to their shoes.

639. Camp shoes are another 'luxury' item you might consider. If you're in the cold then down booties for camp can pack down small and keep you toasty warm, but in the desert it might just some be some light flip-flops or a pair of those free slippers you get from hotels.

640. When it comes to tent mates, it's great to share with people you know, but even better to share with people who either take too much food or don't eat it all. When I was doing the Beyond the Ultimate Ice Ultra, I just lay by the bin and ate any scraps people were throwing away.

641. Never underestimate the power of a favourite snack for motivational emergencies.

642. When putting together your food list for each day, there is usually a required number of calories as a minimum. While this is the way to keep your pack as light as possible, it doesn't matter how light your pack is if you don't have the energy to move forward.

643. One study by Kate Edwards and her team, looking at athletes doing multi-day ultras, found that all their participants ended up in exercise-induced ketosis, so were fully out of carbs and utilising a high percentage of stored body fats. At this point it's normally the most effective way to fuel yourself anyway, but it's like being in first gear as you just can't go above a certain effort threshold.

Urban trails races are becoming more popular, especially in hilly towns like Lyon. © Tim Lloyd

644. To avoid completely emptying the tank is a mixture of packing the right foods, but also getting your effort level right too. At lower effort levels we all use higher percentages of body fat as fuel, with a lower percentage coming from muscle glycogen and carbs we put into the body. It can be a fine balance, but if you work at a level that's right, you can at least hold off exercise-induced ketosis and work at a higher effort level for a bit longer.

645. If you want to find out more about what fuel you're burning then get yourself into a lab for physiological testing and try to replicate the conditions you're going to race in, as these might change the situation too, as will the days of racing beforehand in the real situation.

646. Think about the carbs you'll need for fuel each day, but also for refuelling at night. It'll likely not be possible to start each day with full glycogen stores, but we can at least try. No running around at camp either; keep everything ticking over easy when you're not racing, as you need to save those carbs.

647. If you're cold, then get close to other people and keep warm together. If they're not your friends, hope they're cold too and have the same idea. Always ask first though.

648. Want to go the extra mile in testing your food, then make it more real. Arctic Circle? Put your food in the freezer before a long run to see how it goes. Desert? Roll your sandwich in a sandbox and see if you still like it.

649. Most multi-day races these days have online or WhatsApp groups for those involved to get to know each other first. Make the most of these, but don't listen to the one chump saying they're doing 300 kilometres a week with a backpack on. Do your thing and train smart.

650. If you do know people who have done the race before, then it could be worth asking to borrow or buy some of the more expensive kit such as rucksacks, sleeping bags, emergency beacons or snow shoes.

651. There's also the option of renting equipment, as many do for big expeditions into the Himalaya and the like. If you're only going to use the kit once and then chuck it in the attic to rot, you might as well save a few quid.

652. If you don't fancy getting second-hand kit (you're going to be sleeping in a big smelly tent with people who have rotting feet so get used it) and really want to buy new, then maybe consider what to do with the kit you won't use again. Reselling is great and there's bound to be someone who could use that lightweight sleeping bag after you.

653. Don't just buy a first-aid kit online and never even look inside. Think about what you might actually use, what you're likely to run out of and build up a good first-aid kit over time. Mine has been to many places and not been used that often, but it's full of bits I might actually need so I'm happy to carry it with me.

Don't have fancy hills to practise on? Go and find some stairs to practise those fast feet on. © Tim Lloyd

HOW TO RUN AN ULTRA (654–689)

654. I'll start by quoting the great US ultra-runner Ann Trason: 'ultra-marathons are just an eating and drinking competition with a little bit of running thrown in'. Keep that in mind throughout this section and your ultra-marathon.

655. If you do get into ultra-running, then build up gradually. Each race becomes part of your experience and learning for the next step. Your 50K is a long run for your 50-miler, which helps you with your first 100K. A handful of 50-milers or 100K races will build you up to your first 100-miler.

656. It's not just the 10- to 16-week block of training before your ultra that counts, it's the months and years before that too.

657. The fastest way to the finish of an ultra is not always about moving quickly forward. Chew on that one for a bit.

658. The longer the ultra-marathon is, the less it becomes about physical fitness, and the greater role other factors play. Your fitness signifies your potential, not your performance.

659. Some, but not all, of these key areas of ultra-running are: fitness, specificity (aligning your training with the demands of the event you're preparing for), mental toughness, fuelling, pacing, downhill running, using hiking poles, kit choice, sense of humour and the ability to prevent chafing.

660. If you'd struggle to laugh at yourself when you fall over in a large cowpat or if you cramp up when you climb over a stile, then think long and hard about entering an ultra-marathon.

661. When dealing with road-based ultras, it's very much about the distance itself, whereas for trail and mountain ultras you need to take into account the elevation and technicality of the trail. Doing a 50K on road is 50K, but 50K on rocky trails with 3,000 metres of elevation might take you twice as long and actually be the equivalent of a flatter 80K or an 100K for you.

662. Do your research before you race. Be it simply the race website, the elevation profile, last year's results and pictures or even reading people's blogs or looking for videos.

663. Have a plan A, B and C and continue as far as you can down the alphabet. You need adaptability for ultra-running, and even a perfect day involves some stuff going wrong sometimes. Be prepared for as many situations as you can, then you'll be better prepared for the unexpected too.

664. Expect the ups and downs. Ultra-running can be a rollercoaster ride, from race to race, hour to hour or even kilometre to kilometre. If you accept that the low times will come, then you can remind yourself that the good times always come back too, even if only brought on by a finish line. It can't keep getting worse.

665. Troubleshoot low moods with logical causes. Nine times out of ten it'll be down to low energy, dehydration, overheating, poor pacing or worrying too much about things you can't control, like other runners. Deal with the things you can impact, put a smile on your face and accept that some people will have better days (or are simply better runners on the day) and you can only focus on doing your best.

666. They say you should 'beware the chair', but for some a quick sit down to sort out everything can have a very positive impact. Know yourself; and if you're likely to sit in a chair and never get out again, then don't. I once saw a man sit in a folding chair halfway through a 100-miler, get his finger caught and lose the tip of it. The result was a DNF and a hospital visit. Beware of that chair in particular.

667. Deal with problems before they become disasters. Ignore a hot spot and it'll become a blister and before you know it your foot has melted together with your shoe and you have to wear it for the rest of your life.

668. Sore nipples affect us all, so don't ignore them either. If you're a female runner, make sure you've got a sports bra that you know can do the distance without chafing. Chaps, you can wear a sports bra if you like (some have handy extra pockets too), but a secure plaster or tape will do the job too. A second of pain to remove tape post-race is better than a lifetime without nipples. Or 50 kilometres of running with two red lines running down your top and scaring all the kids.

669. At checkpoints, be quick, but don't rush. If you need a few extra seconds to take another sandwich or wait for a hot drink, then think of it as time invested in the next section of the race, rather than time wasted.

670. Always say please and thank you at checkpoints, and smile, even if you feel like absolute trash. If racing abroad, learn what please and thank you are in the local language. The smile you get back will lighten the load on your feet.

RACING (555–719)

671. Volunteering at races yourself is not only a wonderful experience as part of the ultra-running community, but you'll learn from it too. At the early checkpoints you'll see mistakes to avoid making, like charging through and dropping all your jelly babies because you're rushing. In the middle you'll see the difference between those who rushed and those with big smiles and at later checkpoints you'll learn lessons from everyone on how to cope.

672. Watch those striving to beat the cut-offs. The ones who have to give it everything on race day just to make it before the little hand meets the big hand at midnight. They will fill your heart with inspiration and teach you as many lessons as those at the front.

673. If you're allowed a drop bag at the halfway point then make sure it's nice and visible and put your name and number on. It'll help you or the checkpoint staff spot it.

674. Plan what you might need and add a couple of extras, just in case things aren't going to plan (remember they probably won't be, but that's okay). Fresh socks take time to put on, but can make it feel like you're running on fluffy clouds for a while.

675. If you're running into the night, even if it's warm, it's worth changing into a dry top and/or crop top. The sweat from the day can soak your clothing and it'll cool you down a lot quicker at night. Add in the fact that you might be going a bit slower, so producing less heat, and it can mean trouble. A fresh top has been proven to have a psychological boost too — watch any professional football or rugby team and they generally have fresh kit for the second half for precisely this reason.

676. Plan for disaster and always have enough to scrape through without your drop bag, just in case it doesn't make it. The same goes for your support crew. Anything could happen, or they can just nod off, so have an emergency energy gel or two tucked away so you make it to the next meeting point.

677. Don't get caught in the trap of thinking you're nearly there. At 80 kilometres of a 100K you're 80 per cent done in terms of distance, but if you've slowed down then that last 20 kilometres can take you 30 per cent of your total time if you're not careful.

678. Keep eating until the end. Even in the last 20 or 30 minutes you can hit the wall, as you've been on a knife-edge for hours. Then you take a wrong turn or have underestimated the distance left and it becomes a bit of a mission.

679. If you're racing on trails and your watch says 100 miles and you can't see the finish, don't just sit on the floor and certainly don't angrily (or passive aggressively) tell the race director that it was 101.5 miles according to your watch. You won't be the first, nor the last, and they've probably been awake for over 24 hours trying to put out thousands of different, tiny fires that allowed you to run those miles as safely as possible. Just count those extra miles as 'free miles' as you only paid for 100.

680. In a point-to-point race, remember that every step brings you closer to the finish line. The harder it gets, the more you need to focus on that. Keep moving and you will get there. Keep eating and you might even enjoy some of it.

681. No matter how much you swear you'll never do it again, you will sign up for another race. Normally within a matter of days. Sometimes hours.

682. Your mind treats ultra-marathons like torture. It copes by storing the pain and suffering in the short-term memory, but will store the elation of finishing in the long-term bank and ultimately that's all you'll really remember when looking back with your rose-tinted glasses.

683. If you've got the ultra-running bug, but can't afford to go running big races in the Alps every week, then check out the LDWA. The Long Distance Walkers Association is a wonderful organisation run by volunteers and they have a brilliant community and a whole range of back-to-basics events that don't cost an arm and a leg. Check whether running is allowed for the event beforehand, as some are for walkers only, be respectful of walkers on the day and think of yourself as an ambassador for the rest of us runners too.

684. LDWA navigation is often by written route description, so it's good navigation practice, and over the years I've had some cracking home-made cakes at the checkpoints. Just try to figure out what 'LT at PSB, X field and AH for 300m thru old Gt' means!

685. Don't dismiss walking long distances as part of your training either. When it comes to an ultra, even the front runners will do some walking and hiking along the route, so it's best to include some in your training too.

686. If you're looking to build your experience of time on your feet or just to try out a longer night-time adventure, then a decent length walk will allow you to practise navigating, fuelling and moving at night, without the load on the muscles that an equivalent time or distance running would bring.

687. When you do walk, walk with purpose. A solid walk can often be just as fast as a slow run, especially if you've got your head up, are driving your arms back and you're on a mission. A slow saunter doesn't really help anyone though.

688. A wise man once told me that if you think you should be doing something, chances are you should. This goes for running easier, eating more, stopping to sort out a blister, checking your map or route, smiling more, stopping for a pee and a whole host of other things.

689. If you do need a wee and you're holding it off to save time, remember that you're likely to avoid drinking in this time too and you might end up dehydrated. If water is just gushing straight through you, it could be to do with your electrolyte balance as well.

24-HOUR RUNNING
(690–708)

690. A world unto itself – 24-hour running is my own favourite form of self-flagellation and discovery. Want to really learn what you're made of? Try running around in a small circle for 24 hours just to see how far you can go.

691. It breaks ultra-running down into its simplest parts. Just running and eating. The average pace of a good 24-hour distance never seems that impressive, until you're 18 hours in and struggling to think of a good reason to take that next step.

692. It isn't just about big distances though, anyone can get involved in 24-hour running, and plenty do. It's about going as far as you can in one day; completing even one 24-hour event will change your perspective on a whole lot of different things.

693. Whereas set-distance races mean every step is a step closer to the finish, in a timed event, such as a 48- or 24-hour, it doesn't matter if you're sprinting or sitting on the floor in a puddle of your own tears, you're still getting to the finish line at the same rate. You really must motivate yourself to keep trying your best and for that reason alone it breaks some of the best. There simply is no respite from the push forward.

694. Look forward to changing direction. During a 24-hour race it's important to keep things positive and a chance to see everyone's faces for half a lap and smile at everyone is not to be missed.

695. Get yourself a support crew. If you're serious about running your best 24-hour race then a crew can really make a big difference.

696. It might seem like a lot to ask someone to stand on the side of a 400-metre track handing you biscuits for a full day, but it can also be an opportunity for a friend or family member to really get involved with your sport and they could really enjoy the experience. Ask your Mum or Dad and they might jump at the chance.

697. It could be that no one can commit to the full race, but two or three people could do shifts and cover the full event for you. If this is the case, make sure there is a chance for everyone to chat beforehand, online or in the pub. You can buy the drinks as a pre-race thank you.

698. Plan your nutrition and put it in a sensible format so that your crew can easily see what's in it and with enough information to adapt if they need to. If you have an hourly target for grams of carbohydrates then work out how much is in the myriad of food options you have and make a list, so it's easier for crew to do the maths each hour and make sure you're on target.

699. Have an hourly minimum target for your carbohydrates, but a maximum target for your pace. Going too fast at the start, or not eating enough, both leave you in trouble at hours 12 to 16.

700. Work with your crew on a technique for handing over food and drink. If you're slowing down and speeding up again repeatedly it can have an impact on your muscular fatigue. Make things easier by using little cups or containers to pass over a handful of small items, instead of just throwing them all over the place.

701. Feel free to pace like Yiannis Kouros, Aleksandr Sorokin or Camille Herron (faster from the start) but remember that, for the majority of people, a more evenly paced race is a better idea. If you like to suffer then maybe it'll work for you. You need a good reason to keep going when it all goes to pot though, a really good reason.

702. Starting more conservatively works well for a number of reasons: eating and keeping in some sort of energy balance is easier, you're less likely to trash your legs and when everyone slows in the second half and you slow down less, you'll get the psychological boost of passing all those people who are imploding.

You can run in any weather – skin is waterproof – but make sure you've got a jumper waiting for you at the summit finish.   © *Robbie Britton*

703. If you start sensibly and still have a horrible race, it isn't because you started too slowly. It's more likely something else you're getting wrong. Unless you are called Aleksandr Sorokin, in which case I apologise for ever suggesting you should pace differently as you are now a world record holder.

704. Don't give up on the first try. Or the second and third. There's no getting away from the fact that 24-hour running is really, really hard, but when you get it right it is something special. I might be biased given it's my jam, but there's something very special about it.

705. When training for 24-hour events, you don't need to just run loads of long, slow kilometres. My best results, and those of the people I coach as well, have come from consistency, variation and a good taper.

706. A good, long run in the build-up could be a 100K or 100-miler in the spring with the 24-hour race in the autumn; don't feel like you have to do any mega distances in the traditional 12- to 16-week build-up for your race.

707. If you can come out the other side of a five- or six-hour training run without feeling in bits the next week (good pacing, kit, fuelling and hydration can help), then it can be a useful run in the build-up, but it'll be the biggest single outing I'd advise, otherwise you might still be recovering come race day.

708. Your potential on the start line will come from a combination of your fitness and other factors (rested at the start, fuelling during the race, pacing, and so on) so try to include all of these in your build-up and don't just focus on doing all the running while only eating olives.

High five at The Grizzly in Devon.   © Pete Aylward, RunPhoto

RACING (555-719)

FKTs (709-719)

709. If you're going for the FKT (fastest known time) on a route, as all the cool kids are doing these days, then it can be easier to set one on a route without much history. Ideally a trail opened in the last few years with few record attempts, like Dan and I did on the Jordan Trail in 2019. Or as Amy Sproston did when she broke our record in 2020.

710. Do your research though. Not finding out about faster times in the past, or just because they're not in some self-appointed big almanac of global marks, doesn't mean they don't exist. Be careful; before runners used the acronym FKT, people used to set records. These records are exactly the same thing and you'll be wise to look into them as well, especially in the UK. If I have to come and tell you about a fastest time on a route that you're shouting about then I won't be happy. Peter Bakwin and Buzz Burrell's FKT website is a good resource too (*www.fastestknowntime.com*).

711. In the US they have FKTs for any distance, not just ultras, as has traditionally been the case in the UK. The rule, as defined by Peter and Buzz, is 'the route must be notable and distinct enough so that others will be interested in repeating it' and it needs to be at least five miles (eight kilometres) long or have 500 feet of climbing. Basically, it has to be hilly or interesting, or both.

712. If you're going for a record, it's best to find out if you even have a chance in hell of breaking it. If the FKT currently stands at nine days, and you can't maintain the pace required to beat this for 50K, then chances are you can't do it.

713. Be reasonable with your timeline. It's an FKT, so you get to choose when you do it. There's no need to rush if you're still growing into the athlete who can achieve these goals.

714. Planning is half the battle with FKTs, especially as the routes get longer. Plan as much as you can to make the record attempt as easy as possible. Even if you're unsupported you can plan your timing, kit, resupplying at shops, where water taps are and where you can sleep.

715. If you're going supported – my favourite option as it means you can go faster – then build a good team around you. The running community is full of good people who are willing to help out, so don't be afraid to ask widely for help, but also build a core team of people you trust.

716. Find a route that's interesting to you, not just something you think you can run a fast time on. The months of planning, the organisation and the hard later kilometres will be easier if you're really motivated by the adventure itself.

717. Plan splits and times, but don't be tied down to them. You might be having a better or worse day than planned, but what's important is to do what's right for you at that particular time.

718. If you want to make a fuss on social media and document it in other ways, then make that someone else's role. As a runner, you need to focus on the running, and any tasks that are added to your workload can slow you down.

719. It's best to start in the morning, as each night of missed or reduced sleep will slow you down, and if you can choose when the gun goes off then make it work best for you. The idea of doing a night of running in the dark while you're still fresh doesn't work because adenosine will still build up and cause a foggy, sleepy feeling (see *tips 538–554* on sleep deprivation).

Running can take you to some fantastic places with your friends in tow, like hidden *wadis* (valleys) in Jordan. © *James Vincent*

Tie your laces properly, but be wary of doing them too tight as you can hurt the top of your feet.   © *Tim Lloyd*

007

KIT AND EQUIPMENT
(720–829)

*'The most important bit of technology you have
is the one between your ears.'*

KIT AND EQUIPMENT (720–829)

CLOTHING (720–757)

720. Start from the most important place, your feet, and work your way up. Comfortable shoes trump all the marketing and rubbish you might see in adverts or sponsored social media posts from your favourite runner. It might be tempting to get straight into the fanciest new run-faster kicks, but it's best to ease in and focus on being comfortable first.

721. You don't need to have gait analysis to get started but, if you want to, be sure to do your research and work with people who know what they're talking about, be it a specialist such as Profeet in London, or the local running shop that has an employee who really knows their stuff. Be wary of some of the bigger outlets, where you might just find yourself with someone who's done 30 minutes' training and can only recommend one of two different (insert brand of your choice) shoes.

722. With comfort in first place, the next most important factor for shoes is either grip or weight. If you're running on trails or wet conditions then go for grip first, because you want them to stay rubber-side down. If you're racing in dry road conditions then the weight should be considered, but beyond a certain point you'll be sacrificing comfort and it's important to find the right balance for you.

723. Lightweight shoes are important too, but not to the detriment of other factors entirely. It's a balance, but I'd be lying if I said I hadn't been bamboozled by an incy, wincy, polka-dot pair of shoes occasionally. The lightest of all shoes are track and cross-country spikes, but they definitely take some getting used to and aren't for everyone. If I started using spikes for all my sessions, I think my Achilles would explode.

724. Fancy carbon-plated shoes dominate the market to some extent at the moment, so we need to talk about them. They will make you run faster so, if you want an easy PB, then spend the dollars, but be aware they are not cheap. You can also get faster by training and following the tips in this book, but you can have your cake and eat it by doing that as well as buying carbon-plated shoes.

725. If you're getting serious, consider having racing and training shoes; one might be more lightweight, expensive and, well, faster, but the other is more durable, comfortable and maybe a bit cheaper. Even the rotation between just a couple pairs of shoes can help prevent injury.

726. Keep an eye out for decent deals on shoes, but second-hand shoes can be a good shout too. Your favourite kicks might be just the wrong size for someone else and you can rehouse a 'pre-loved' pair for half the price of new ones.

727. As ReRun Clothing say, a pair of running shoes takes around 1,000 years to decompose, so nearly every single pair ever made still exists on this planet in one form or another. Bear this in mind if you're constantly buying new shoes – the most sustainable bit of kit is the one you already own.

728. You don't need to replace your shoes every 800 kilometres, no matter what any of the big brands say. Of course they want you to believe that, because it's their business to sell you shoes, but some shoes last for ages and you can repair them, relegate them to slippers or garden shoes or make them into a plant pot. Some shoes last way less than 800 kilometres too, because they're rubbish.

Volunteers are a vital part of the running community; the Saturday morning parkrun wouldn't happen without them. © Pete Aylward, RunPhoto

729. Next up, get some decent socks. There's plenty out there, but why spend all that cash on shoes, watches, designer baseball caps and then scrimp on the main point of contact between your skin and the kit? I prefer reasonably well-fitted, ankle-high socks with pretty colours; my main advice is to just avoid cheap and nasty socks. It's rumoured that blister pain is equal to napalm.

730. Going up, the next step is your calves. So, do you need compression calf guards? No. Next question.

731. Shorts come in a multitude of sizes and the general rule of thumb is that the shorter they are, the faster you look. Once again, comfort matters, whether male or female, as there's plenty that can rub in the inner thigh region, and it can get really messy.

732. GB ultra-runner Sarah Cameron recommends that female runners look for shorts with a wider waistband, as normal, narrow elasticated waistbands can dig into your hips and are not that comfortable.

733. Personally, I'm a fan of specific running pants, built to keep things where they're supposed to be and prevent some of that chafing. Again, the c-word – comfort – comes into play. Like socks, it's an area you don't want too much friction.

734. Some shorts come with built-in liners and half tights and if these work for you, then great. Whatever undercarriage plan you go for, test it out before race day, as chafing in the groin region will derail any PB attempt.

735. Shorts with pockets are better, so it's best to start out down that path early doors. Whether it's energy gels, door keys or a little packet of toilet roll *(tips 947–948)*, a bit of storage is good for training and racing.

736. It depends on the season you're starting and where you live, but if it's a 'new year, new you' endeavour, then you might be beginning your running journey while wearing tights or leggings, rather than shorts. For the sake of your friends, family and neighbours, if you're a bloke then wear something over the tights. It's apparently fashionable in London to wear shorts and tights together, but otherwise frowned upon by old-school club runners. Make your own mind up, but be aware of what's on show.

737. When buying shorts and tights, be wary of white. They won't stay white for long anyway. Dan Lawson brought a pair of white running shorts to Jordan on our adventure, and they were considered a biohazard by day four.

738. Continuing up, we get to T-shirts. As a man, the main thing you'll be worrying about with any T-shirt is 'Will this top eat my nipples by kilometre 25?' We've all seen those people finishing marathons with a red line from each nipple; you can't tape your nips for every run.

739. Sports bras are also very important and there's lots of them out there. This might be a good time to go on Facebook and ask for advice, look at reviews and speak to your peers, as the teenage boy working in your local shop might not have much experience. There are a few that have additional storage pockets so, for me, that's a win. I'd even consider wearing one if I needed the pockets.

740. T-shirt material matters, and cheap, plastic tops are prime suspects for chafing and smelling really funky after one run. As with anything, do your research and only get a couple of decent tops, as you'll likely build up a collection of race tops too over the years.

741. Talking of race tops, as a running community we are trying to reduce how many we have, and repurpose what we already have but don't use, via great initiatives like ReRun Clothing and Trees not Tees, but we know people do love to celebrate some of their favourite races so plan those tops into your future and use the ones you already have. If you're not going to wear your Bognor Regis Marathon top, then opt out and save the world from another item in landfill. (For more on sustainability see *tips 758–780*.)

> **742.** Look into different materials. Some of my favourite tops are long-sleeved merino wool numbers. Not only do they avoid stinking after a few runs, they are versatile in terms of weather conditions, keep you warm even when wet and a good one can last you years.

743. For the summer you might want a vest, because they make you look faster and you can tan your arms, but make sure they don't rub around the armpit as it's another sensitive area.

744. If you want real versatility then get some arm sleeves. Cold arms? No problem. Hot arms? Also no problem. Can be worn with a T-shirt or vest and in dire situations can also be used to keep packets of fruit pastilles safe for emergencies. Or keys.

745. Talking of versatility, how about a Buff®, tube or neck gaiter? (Whatever we're allowed to call those bits of material that keep your neck warm.) They're fantastic – they can double up as a face mask, be worn in hundreds of different ways and dunked in water if it's roasting hot too.

746. Hats, caps, bandanas and headbands will all make you look cooler, apparently, but are also good for keeping unruly hair at bay and out of your eyes. Wearing a cycling cap while running is, unfortunately, illegal in 143 countries so not worth the risk.

Photos of runners tying their laces are popular with photographers. © *Tim Lloyd*

747. If you're like me then any pair of running glasses will steam up, but some less than others. If you need your spectacles to see where you're going then a good few brands, such as Julbo and Adidas, will fit prescription lenses into their shades.

748. Try to clean your shades every now and again or you'll run into a tree. If they're not the fancy ones that change in low light, then maybe take them off in the woods. No one should wear sunglasses at night either, but there are clear specs for keeping your eyes safe.

749. Jackets can either be breathable or waterproof. Both is very rare. You'll either get soaked by the rain or soaked by your own sweat – it's a two-pronged attack from the elements. If you find a jacket that does both then let the world know. It's the Holy Grail, but they do exist.

750. A lightweight, windproof jacket is one of the most versatile items in anyone's arsenal. Some pack up small enough to fit in a pocket or can be wrapped around your waist. More breathable than a waterproof, they can stop a harsh wind from wicking away all your heat, but will also save your bacon in a storm if you just need to keep warm while still moving, as they trap some heat in too.

751. Waterproof jackets are needed if you're out for a longer time, especially in the hills. If you're just out for an hour or so on a local training run, you can probably keep warm enough by just actually running (or moving) for the whole run and then dry out back at home.

752. If you'll be out all day in a race or on a training outing and it's persisting it down, then there are decent jackets that will keep you dry. As long as you don't get too sweaty underneath: then you'll be wet anyway.

753. Most waterproofs don't work well against skin, so always have a long-sleeved top (or those fancy arm sleeves) underneath.

754. Unless you live in Antarctica or intend to race in some extreme environments, a down jacket or gilet has no place in your running kit. Either work harder, so you don't get cold, or get something synthetic that won't lose all warming capabilities when soaked with your sweat. The one exception to this rule is Daniel Alan Lawson, who is in fact a cold-blooded lizard and needs a down jacket to run in all but the hottest conditions.

755. Gloves are good at keeping your hands warm, but mittens are better. A good pair of running gloves will suffice if your body is still warm too, but in cold conditions you shunt the blood away from your extremities, and they get cold first. Windproof or waterproof gloves can be really useful, but again be wary of getting too sweaty underneath. The best waterproof gloves are Marigolds, but they do get a little sweaty.

756. It keeps cropping up, but with kit, comfort really is king (or queen). If you're comfortable then you can run to the best of your ability. If you're looking for those extra boosts from lightweight kit and shoes, think about the balance with comfort, as a four per cent improvement due to lighter shoes might be outweighed by a larger decrease due to waddling the last few kilometres with chafing and massive blisters.

757. Except for shorts. Those really are just shorter equals faster. Until they become briefs and you look like Lance Armstrong doing a triathlon. Not cool, kids.

SUSTAINABILITY (758–780)

758. As a runner you're most likely already quite in tune with the environment, especially if you love running on the trails, but we can all do our bit. Our environmental impact runs through every aspect of our lives, so here's some ways to think about it within our sport.

759. The most sustainable bit of kit is the one you already own. Brands may be advertising pants made out of recycled dog collars, but if you already own some decent pants and don't really need those extra ones, not buying them will lessen your impact.

760. Look at extending the life of your own kit, by looking after it well and repairing it when it does break, if possible.

761. The quality of kit you purchase matters too. Cheaper, poorly made kit won't last you as long, so it's a bit of a false economy.

762. Look into how your kit is made and the ethical standards of the company you're buying from. The *Ethical Consumer* website (***www.ethicalconsumer.org***) gives you the low-down on a lot of the big players and it never hurts to educate yourself.

763. Another thing to look for is a closed-loop recycling plan. A brand takes back what they produce after its intended lifespan and then reuse the materials themselves. This amounts to a brand taking responsibility for what they produce, even after it's gone to the consumer.

764. Running trainers take around 1,000 years to decompose, so nearly every single trainer ever made is still on the planet. Ideally brands would take responsibility for what happens to that shoe after you've finished using it, but you can try to extend the useful life of your own trainers as much as possible.

765. You often hear that shoes last 500 miles (800 kilometres); I've even seen 300 miles (480 kilometres) quoted. Then your injury risk rises because the shoe is breaking down, but it's not as simple as just binning them as they hit that mark. I've had shoes last me well over 1,500 kilometres, but some last a lot less too.

766. Fellow coach Gary House has a great quote about when to replace your trainers, but just in case the kids have got hold of this book, let's just say it's 'when they're kippered'. There are a few things you can do to try and repair your running shoes but, if they literally fall to pieces, that's a good sign they're gone.

767. Look at the tread pattern on your shoes. Not only will it give you a good insight into how you run, but also how much you can keep using those shoes. Ideally the sole, which is the surface grinding into the ground at every step, is what eventually wears out.

768. If the soles of your favourite shoes wear out but the uppers are still holding strong, then your local cobbler, or a specialist such as Lancashire Sports Repairs, can replace the soles for you. Brand new Vibram soles can keep those bad boys going for a fair few more kilometres.

769. If the upper is gone, it's usually in a few common places: where the little toe pokes out of the side or the crease along your toes or the heel cup. A well-fitted shoe might be less likely to break down in those places, but also look for kicks with reinforcement where you know you normally smash your shoes up.

You can tell a lot about a runner from the soles of their shoes. These tell us that I don't run in spikes very often. © *Tim Lloyd*

KIT AND EQUIPMENT (720-829)

770. ReRun Clothing is a great resource for tips and hacks to prolong your kit life. One of which is using mouldable waterproof lining tape, normally used on the seams of waterproof jackets, to melt onto the holes in your trainers. It'll fit over the gap and maybe give you an extra couple of hundred kilometres on those uppers. Check out *@rerun.clothing* on Instagram.

771. Brands such as Patagonia and Alpkit will repair kit too, as will a local garment repair shop. Broken zips, holes and the like don't need to mean the end of life for a piece of kit. Personally, I think a patch only ever makes something look better.

772. If you want to keep your mementos, but you're not using them, then consider using companies like Gins Running Stitch. They can upcycle or repurpose your favourite race T-shirts into something you will actually use.

773. With race T-shirts being one of the single biggest donations to ReRun Clothing (whose aim is to reduce the amount of waste produced by the running industry), it's clear we're producing too many of them. Yes, finishing your first marathon or ultra and having something to wear that you can show off is great, but soon you'll be piling up ill-fitting and unused tops in the bottom of your cupboard.

774. It's perfectly fine to decline a race T-shirt or a medal at the finish if you don't want or need them. It might be a bit awkward, but if you know you won't wear it then even this little message, if enough of us did this, could make a change.

775. A great option for all race directors is Trees not Tees. The organisation encourages race organisers to give runners the option to choose between a T-shirt they'll never wear or the planting of a tree in Scotland. Set up by celebrated fell and mountain runner Jim Mann, it lets runners and race organisers at least have the choice of a more sustainable action.

776. If you do want to take your race T-shirt, there isn't anything wrong with that. I'm not trying to shame people into refusing them, but look at the quality of it first and really do consider if you'll use it.

777. For female runners, ask if the T-shirt is a female-specific fit because, in reality, 'unisex' just means 'men's fit' still.

778. Sometimes, if a friend or family member has helped me at a race, I will ask them if they would like the T-shirt, and ask for it in their size instead.

779. Remember that just because you take a bag of clothes to the charity shop or send them to ReRun Clothing, it doesn't give you a free pass to buy another load of stuff that you don't need. It's worth repeating: the most sustainable bit of kit is the one you already own.

780. If you do need something new for a race then it can be worthwhile checking out second-hand (or pre-loved) options first.

TECHNOLOGY (781-798)

781. The most important bit of technology you have is the one between your ears.

782. No watch, heart rate monitor or foot sensor can replace your own perception of how you're running; if you find yourself over-reliant on a GPS watch for your pace, or shoes that tell you how to run, then you're not likely to really reach your potential.

783. That said, there is some fine technology out there and it can aid your running and help you improve. It just shouldn't dictate it.

KIT AND EQUIPMENT (720-829)

784. To start with, a GPS watch links up to all the satellites in the sky to tell you how far, how fast and where you're running. They can be great for recording your running and that's just the start.

785. Think about what you want from a watch before spending all your dollars. If you're just going to time each run then it's not worth getting an all-singing, all-dancing adventure model that costs £400. You might as well just check the clock on your cooker before you head out.

786. A basic stopwatch has its merits, as you can tell the time and time your runs. For my first few 24-hour races, it was all I used. It was only a sponsorship deal that made me swap to a proper GPS watch and even then, for 24-hour racing, I still only used the stopwatch on that.

787. The more you spend, the more features you get, but this doesn't actually directly correspond to how useful the watch is or how much faster it'll make you. Bonus tip: the watch won't make you faster, you have to do that yourself.

788. The basic functions of recording your run route and paces can be done with an app on your phone, but for the sake of not having to carry your phone everywhere, I'd recommend a low-end GPS watch for those wanting to progress in their running.

789. Back in the day, I did use a piece of string and a map to mark out how long certain loops were near my home. That way I could build my training log and do some kilometre reps or a tempo run that I knew was a certain distance. It was the cheapest way to do things.

790. Now there are great apps such as Komoot, which allow you to plan a route, on a laptop or on your phone, and you can measure how far you'll be running without any string at all. Except for your laces.

791. Think about what you want from the watch and what type of running you want to do. If you want to do ultras in the future, then think about battery life. It's no good if your watch runs out halfway round the race and you need to show off on Strava afterwards.

792. Check out the navigation ability of the watch if you want to go further afield too. If you can download a route from an app like Komoot on to your watch then it's brilliant for visiting new places, even just on a weekend break to a new city.

793. Additionally, a lot of watches have 'breadcrumb' settings so you can follow your route back to where you started. This is great for those times when you insist you're not lost, right up until the point that you have absolutely zero idea where you are! It's a good idea to test the breadcrumb setting out before you actually need it, instead of relying on being able to use it when you actually need to and finding out you had to press something at the start.

794. Heart rate monitors are a really handy piece of kit for runners *(tips 114–115)*. These can be uncomfortable for some and, as you can imagine, they were probably initially designed for a man, by a man. There are a couple of sports bras with HR monitors inbuilt that can be a better option for women.

795. If you're using a chest strap HR monitor, make it a little tight at the start of your run as it'll sag a bit when it gets soaked in your sweat.

At night, when tired, you're more likely to make poor decisions, like my beard.   © *James Vincent*

796. Before a run, it's important to moisten the sensors, as the monitor works best when there is a conductive layer between you and the sensor. You can't always count on a layer of sweat being there straight away, so I just lick it. This gets more disgusting depending on how often you wash your HR strap and if you run double days. If regularly licking an incredibly salty HR strap isn't your jam, then a tiny bit of washing-up liquid, or just water from the tap, can do a good job. Just don't use washing-up liquid one day and then lick it the next.

797. Wrist HR monitors are becoming more and more common, but I've yet to use one that is consistently accurate enough for my liking. The best has been 'consistently inaccurate'.

798. If you are using a wrist HR monitor then it needs to be tight on your wrist with no clothing underneath. Use the same wrist each time and be sceptical if it says your heart rate is at 250bpm. Unless you're having a heart attack, in which case call the emergency services.

HEAD TORCHES (799–816)

799. Of all the kit to compromise on to save weight, head torches are the worst option. It's a false economy, especially if running on trails.

800. Finding a head torch that is comfortable for you can be difficult, as it's not easy to try them on beforehand. Maybe go to an outdoor store, as they normally have a bigger range and might have some you can pop on your noggin and bounce around a bit before purchasing.

801. If you have a small head, you find the weight on your skull uncomfortable or it's difficult to manage with bigger hair then some head torches do have the ability to use a battery pack stored on your waist. This is also good in really cold conditions if you're finding batteries drain quickly.

KIT AND EQUIPMENT (720-829)

Sarah Castree on rocky trails in the Lost Valley of Glen Coe.
© Keri Wallace, Girls on Hills – **www.girlsonhills.com**

802. Some runners like to attach head torches to their waist, so the beam is naturally lower and offers a different light. These could even be coupled with a smaller head torch on your head so there is still some light when you look around, rather than having to twist your crotch towards the woods when you hear a noise.

803. Some runners find that wearing a bandana or headband underneath the head torch can make it more comfortable and stop you dripping sweat just from where it sits on your head. It's no good having a great torch if it just makes salty sweat pour into your eyes.

804. Learn about lumens. If you actually want to see where you're going then the minimum I'd use is 150 lumens. Brighter is better, especially on trails. When you try a brighter head torch you won't go back. It makes a difference to your confidence when running at night, makes you more visible to cars and other trail users and really doesn't feel that different on your head.

805. Look for a torch with a wide beam as, if the beam is too narrow, it feels like you're running down a small hole for the entire run. It can even give some people a headache or nausea.

806. If your head torch is rechargeable, rather than battery-powered, you won't be able to use it for some mountain races as you are required to carry a spare battery.

807. Test different settings as this can heavily influence battery life. You might not need the maximum level of lumens for that street-lit road, so either get one of the Reactive Lighting beauties from Petzl, which use a sensor to adjust the beam brightness and pattern, or figure out how to adjust yours on the fly.

808. If I'm racing at night and someone next to me has a real beast of a head torch, I might turn mine off going uphill. It'll save your batteries but comes with some risks – if they turn their head off the trail they will leave you in the pitch black. They'll also realise you're using their light, but then just blame this book.

809. Turn your head torch off when you go into checkpoints. They're usually well-lit and you'll just blind everyone trying to help you out. If you do forget to turn your head torch off at a checkpoint, and aren't instantly reminded by everyone shielding their eyes and ducking away from you, then consider that you might be low on blood sugar and get some food in. We make poor decisions when we're under-fuelled and tired.

810. Keep your spare batteries warm. There's nothing worse than getting stuck in the dark, going for your extra juice and it's drained in the cold.

811. Have a backup torch handy, so you can use it if you have to find your spare batteries and it's pitch black. You can't always count on there being extra light around for those tasks and trying to find your spare torch or a spare battery becomes a real pain.

812. Double check that your batteries are fully charged before racing or running at night; don't just leave them on charge overnight and grab them before you go. All it takes is a loose cable to slow charging or a bad connection to mean no charging at all.

813. Learn about the red light on your torch too. Sometimes if there is enough ambient light for me to see where I'm going, I'll spin the torch round on my head and use the red light as an extra bit of security to make me more visible to cars approaching from behind. It can also be useful for reading shiny things, like a map, if your light is too bright.

814. When running with a friend side by side on a country lane, if you both have good head torches then approaching cars will assume you're another car and the level of respect given can increase. When the car passes, one of you has to pretend to be the driver with an imaginary steering wheel.

815. If it gets foggy or you're in low cloud then hold your torch closer to the ground, even if this means taking it off your head for a while. At head height it's likely the full beam will just be reflected into your face and that won't really help. Point it at the ground ahead from a lower angle and you'll see more of the important stuff, like rocks and tree roots. If pointing your head torch at the ground in fog, or just if you're generally focused on the trail ahead, make sure you don't run into low-hanging tree branches or bridges. This is obviously more of a problem for tall people.

816. Bonus tip for giants with small friends: if you run with a smaller friend, don't just assume you'll fit under the branch ahead because they did. Many a time I've taken a lanky chum for a run and they've moaned that I didn't warn about a low-hanging branch. Well, it wasn't a problem in my stunted world.

KIT AND EQUIPMENT (720-829)

HIKING POLES (817-829)

817. Hiking poles can really improve your efficiency in mountain ultras, but be aware they are banned in hill races in Scotland. Apparently this goes back to a fourteenth-century law about arming Highland warriors with pointy sticks. In reality, this is partly down to the environmental damage poles can have on trails, so do be cautious of this. You're increasing the width of your impact, but also striking the ground with a metal or rubber tip. If a conservation area asks you not to use them, or you're off-trail, then do consider the impact of their use.

818. Technique is important; if I had 50 pence for every British or US runner I saw just tapping the poles alongside them to very little effect I actually would have thousands of pounds. Do some research, check out some YouTube videos and practise.

819. I'm a fan of double poling (moving both poles forward at the same time) when going uphill, with a slight delay in the time between the poles touching down. You want them to land slightly ahead of you, and then drive through with your arms until you have pushed yourself forward. Another way to think about it is imagining you have roller skates on your feet and you are dragging yourself uphill via the poles. Don't forget to use your legs in the actual races though.

820. The other style is using them alternately as your arms go forward, and this works for some. It's the same idea as the 'diagonal stride' in cross-country skiing; there are a couple of good cross-country skiing apps and videos that demonstrate pole technique better than any hiking video I've seen thus far.

821. When using hiking poles, you're asking a lot of your arms, so you need to train them up beforehand to get the most out of your poles. It's an endurance exercise; just having good technique and getting your poles out on race day will likely leave you pretty kippered by halfway round if your arms aren't strong enough.

822. Some runners use poles downhill too, like wizards of the trail. If you're one of these people, can you let us all know how you learned this skill? I think it's probably down to years of using them, especially when hiking too. If you're not too skilled at using poles downhill, or just downhill running in general, then it's risky adding extra limbs into the equation.

823. If things get ugly with your quads in a race, then poles can help relieve some of the pressure on the descents, but will likely slow you down if used pre-emptively. Try to become more efficient in your downhill running in general, with or without poles, with purposeful practice.

824. If you use wrist loops, then learn how to use them properly. Hold the loop in the air and then slot your hand through and drop the loop on to your wrist. The idea is that force is applied to the strap, not through gripping the pole. If you're gripping the pole to apply force when driving through then that's not efficient and the muscles in your forearm will tire out way too quickly.

825. The wee gloves you get with some poles, which clip directly on to the pole, allow for a much better transfer of power, but do sometimes make it harder to eat. Test them out, but make a concerted effort to eat, as there is no use in having an efficient transfer of power if you have no power to begin with.

826. When using poles on trails, be aware of those around you. Knowing when an opponent is going to overtake means you can quickly stab them with your pole to discourage such a discourteous action. Seriously though, stabbing people is bad. Don't do it. Especially if you have the tips that are like little knives to cut into the ground. Be careful of others flailing their poles around too, as it's best to finish an ultra with both eyes intact.

827. Test out where you'll store your poles when not using them. Some packs have storage clips, others can be fitted with a quiver, but make sure it's easy to use or one of two things will happen: you will carry the poles in your hands for the entire race, even when not using them, or you will leave them on your pack for the entirety.

828. Alternatively, a running belt could be used. The Naked® Running Band is one example and it has an easy-to-use pole holder at the back (or the front if you spin it round). Even if you don't have hills near home, it's worth going out for an easy run and taking your poles out, using them for a few steps and then replacing them a number of times. Iron out any issues and make sure that when you're tired it's not a problem. The neighbours already think you're weird, so stop worrying about what they think.

829. Ignore the people who call them 'cheat sticks'. It's not cheating, and in the mountains they can make a huge difference, so why put yourself at a disadvantage?

Hiking poles in action on the Transgrancanaria. © *Pete Aylward, RunPhoto*

The better you get at downhill running, the more you can enjoy the view occasionally. In this instance, the author didn't even realise Mont Blanc was to his left. © *Natalie White*

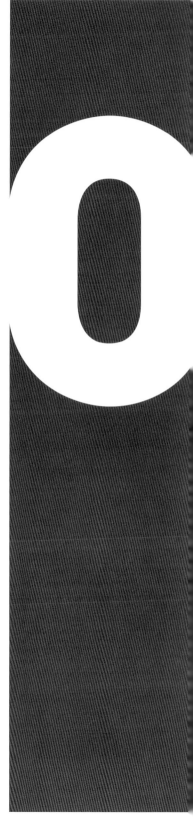

Sometimes what's round the next corner can surprise you, but it's not often as spectacular as Petra. © James Vincent

008

TRAVELLING
(830–911)

*'A silk liner can really increase the warmth of a sleeping
bag without adding too much weight or bulk to your kit.
So can sleeping in all your clothes or camping in a barn.
Or a four-star hotel if it all goes Pete Tong.'*

TRAVELLING (830-911)

TRAINING CAMPS AND ADVENTURES (830-838)

830. A great way to add a bit of extra oomph into your training is through the wonderful thing known as a training camp. Be it a new location in your home country, or somewhere a bit more exotic overseas, they aren't just for elite athletes; everyone can enjoy them.

831. 'Training camp' actually translates into non-running speak as 'holiday with your running friends' so make sure you explain that's it's purely training focused and you're super serious.

832. The biggest impact of any training camp isn't the location, the weather or the facilities, but the people. Yes, it's lovely to be somewhere nice and warm, but if it chucks it down every day (thanks, Portugal) you'll still come out the other side fit as a fiddle if you've got a good training group.

833. With the weather in mind, don't just pack shorts and a vest as even the warmest locations can have adverse weather. One waterproof jacket will probably do.

834. You can go on organised trips, there are plenty about these days, or get together with a group of friends and plan something yourself with bit of research.

835. Look for locations that have a track and gym if you want to include your usual sessions or strength workouts, but also a good selection of roads and trails to run on.

836. Book somewhere with a kitchen so you can share some group meals rather than eating out every night, as that can become expensive and is not the best way to manage your own diet during training.

837. Plan any training camps for the peak weeks of a training block and it can really pay off on race day. If you know your biggest mileage will be five or six weeks out from the race then a week or two of sharing those miles somewhere warm will make those weeks smoother, and also fill you with motivation for the weeks before the taper too.

838. Look for a location that allows you to train specifically for your event. It's no good heading to the warm coast if it's all flat and you have a mountain race coming up, but equally you can't go into the bigger mountains in March due to the snow, so bear that in mind too.

RACING OVERSEAS (839-858)

839. From simply wanting to see a new city on holiday to the optimum PB opportunity, sometimes it's nice to race in different places and it's a great way to experience a new country or culture.

840. There are global race calendars online, especially if you're looking for big city marathons or ultras, but sometimes national websites will be the best place to get something a little different. Get in touch with runners from the country you want to visit to find out where they find all their events.

841. When picking a country to travel to consider the environmental differences too. If you struggle in the heat then a marathon PB attempt in Greece in August might not be a great idea, but alternatives might be placed just at the right time of year to hit your fastest time, such as Valencia or Berlin.

Before any race, a warm-up should include some of the challenges you'll face when the gun goes off.   © *Tim Lloyd*

TRAVELLING (830-911)

Train with someone long enough and you'll mimic their stride, but thankfully not their hair. © Tim Lloyd

842. Speak to club members and friends about travelling to an event together. It can turn a weekend away into a real lifetime memory when shared with friends, and then at least one of you has to have a good race, right?

843. If you book your flight early and find a cheap hotel or hostel, then racing overseas can actually work out cheaper than some events in your own country, although do consider the added environmental impact of the flight. Pay for some trees from Trees not Tees *(tip 775)*, to at least balance it out a little.

844. When booking flights, have a look at where the airport is, especially if you're using a budget airline. There's nothing worse than planning to get in late to avoid too much time off work and then being stuck out in the sticks because London Southend Airport isn't actually anywhere near London.

845. Keep your essentials in your hand luggage. This means shoes, socks, pants, bra, shorts and vest for racing. If there is something you can't replace or do without in the case of lost luggage, then don't even think about putting it in the hold. Even a handful of your favourite energy gels can go in the clear plastic bag and be carried through security. You might be able to get new energy gels at the race expo, but having the ones you've trained with is too important to put at risk.

846. Make a checklist before you travel. It can be on your phone or a bit of scrap paper; anything that you can do to reduce the stress of travelling can help you get to the start line feeling better. Put normal things like 'check-in' and 'pack bag', but also add in your easy run the day before flying and getting your race number and pinning it on to your vest the night before.

847. On the flight an aisle seat is going to be better as you're able to get up and stretch your legs out whenever you want to. Stay well hydrated and your bladder will create a walk schedule for you.

848. Plan ahead for food too. Eating the flight food is fine, but if it's wildly different from what you'd normally eat then better to stick to a plan; a small packed lunch might stop you ordering the massive bag of sweets (unless that's part of your carb-loading plan).

849. While we're talking about flights, remember the importance of sleep in the week before your race, especially if you know you won't get a wink the night before the gun goes off.

850. That 5.30 a.m. flight might be cheaper and get you in at a nice time, but the 4.00 a.m. check-in and the 3.00 a.m. departure from home, coupled with being up late still deciding on which shoes and energy gels to take, means your sleep is going to take a hit.

851. When planning where to stay, look for somewhere close to the start line, especially if it's an early one. Being near the finish might be helpful at the end but it won't have any impact on performance, whereas being near the start can definitely help.

852. Look out for pubs, clubs or anything that might be open late and noisy near to your hotel. I once stayed in a cheap hotel near Geneva airport, next to an arena where there was a rehearsal for a rock concert that went on until gone midnight. Sleep was problematic.

853. Pro tip for getting a good night's sleep: take your own pillowcase with you. It's easy to pack and your face will feel like it's right at home.

854. Earplugs are also a good shout, for flights or staying in a hostel. However, don't wear them on race morning and sleep through your alarm.

855. Save the testing of the local cuisine, especially anything particularly exotic, until after your race. Those Calabrian prawns might look great, but having an upset stomach on race day is no fun.

856. The same goes for sightseeing and race expos. Clocking up miles of walking, likely in the heat of the day, is no way to get your legs ready to race. 'Oh, I'm not running today, so I'll just walk for six hours and get 12 coffees instead', said no one who ran a PB.

857. Learn at least a few words of the local language before going, especially 'thank you'. It's not hard to do and the smile it will bring to a volunteer's face when you say 'graziass' in a Derek Trotter accent is totally worth it. Maybe add 'where is the start?' into your vocabulary too.

858. Get a magnet for your Ma. They love little touches like that and it's a nice memento of where you've been. If your other half or kids are left at home, then get them something too, it means you'll be more likely to be allowed to race overseas the next time.

Food in both hands is the best way to tackle the Transgrancanaria. © *Pete Aylward, RunPhoto*

FASTPACKING (859-874)

859. Fastpacking is a hybrid of trail running and ultra-lightweight backpacking, with a bit of hiking thrown in too. If you're training for a mountain or trail race it can be a good idea to fastpack the route first over several days.

860. Any route that is set up for walkers to enjoy can work really well when fastpacked. One great example is the West Highland Way in Scotland. Both the start, at Milngavie, and the finish, at Fort William, have good rail connections; the route has plenty of accommodation options if you don't want to camp. There's a great fish and chip shop at the halfway point in Tyndrum as well.

861. Pack enough clothes for each day, but also take a light outfit to change into in the evening. This means you can keep your pack light enough that you can run with it, resupplying food and drink along the way.

862. Most great routes have a guidebook or a website that breaks the trail down into segments or legs. As a runner you should be able to cover a bit more than a hiker in a day; make sure that you do your research as some sections may just be rough going for all.

863. Aim to finish each day comfortably, not pushing the limits of your endurance. Paced wisely, a longer trail run split into several days can be a great adventure, but also excellent training. An evening by the fire with a pub meal feels all the more satisfying if you've got there on foot.

864. The UK has a whole host of National Trails that are great for fastpacking, including the Pennine Way and the South Downs Way; there are also many lesser-known trails where you'll need to do a bit of extra planning yourself.

865. Look for hostels and hotels at decent intervals, check multiple websites and maybe just call up some of the local village pubs not listed online. The Youth Hostels Association is always a great shout, but going off-trail for a kilometre or so into a village might open up plenty of hotel and pub options.

866. Even going further afield to well-known and established hiking trails, such as the Tour du Mont Blanc, or one of the race routes popular in Europe, is possible with some planning. Again, err on the side of caution for the length of your days as you're not trying to break any records (this time at least); it's better to have a couple of extra hours at your refuge than getting benighted on the trail.

867. Build up to the bigger adventures in the mountains, and travel with more experienced friends, or even book a guide, who will not only know the trail, but also how to keep you safe.

868. Just as in the UK, you can plan your own trip on lesser-known routes elsewhere too, as I did on the Kom-Emine trail in Bulgaria. A bit of digging can reveal a guidebook, websites or even those with experience of the trail who can help.

869. In Bulgaria I worked with a local guide called Zhivko. He checked the itinerary, helped book some of the more remote mountain huts and eventually I hired him to transport some luggage on the adventure too. He was absolutely brilliant, and without him the whole trip would have been harder, maybe even impossible.

TRAVELLING (830-911)

870. Wherever you are, have someone at home to check in with each evening and a plan for them to follow if they don't hear from you.

871. If you know you're not going to have any signal and you're somewhere a bit more remote, then think about renting a satellite phone or a SPOT device. Gone are the days when personal locator beacons were so big it only made sense to carry them on your boat or in a tank.

872. What you pack will vary based on where you're travelling, but some of the basics are needed wherever you are. Always check the weather forecast, both short- and long-term, and be prepared for it to change if you're out for multiple days. If in doubt, make sure you have enough equipment with you to survive a full day and night out on the trail. A closed refuge or simply getting lost might mean you need to look after yourself and your group for an extended period, so it's best to be suitably equipped.

873. If travelling in a group, it's worth asking each other about first-aid qualifications. If it's likely that you'll be somewhere remote then it's good to have at least one team member with some experience. Sod's law, it'll be the individual who is trained in first aid who will have an accident, so think about at least two of the group having some sort of clue and knowing what's in the first-aid kit. Might as well be you if you're reading this.

874. Look for wilderness or outdoor-specific first-aid courses, rather than basic office ones. A first-aid provider might even run a specific course if enough of you want to sign up, then they can tailor it to include scenarios you're more likely to see in your own adventures.

WHAT TO PACK FOR AN ADVENTURE (875-898)

875. The first thing you need is a pack to carry everything in. The boom in ultra-running and fastpacking has meant this area has seen some great advances in recent years. Many options are available, from race packs that have the capacity to carry three to five litres of kit, as well as water bottles and food, to more specific fastpacking rucksacks that hold 20 to 30 litres, but are still something you can run with.

876. Find a pack that works for you and specifically your adventure. It doesn't have to be brand spanking new and exactly right, but it's better to have a bit of extra room and compress the bag down a bit, rather than something filled to the brim. Halfway round you might find you need an extra jacket, blanket, food or water storage and need that extra space.

877. Test everything before you go, particularly looking at any rubbing or chafing when the pack is full. What would be a little rub over a short run or hike can become a big problem over three or four days.

878. Think about the demands and weather conditions of your adventure and make a list of items you'll need. You can even look at what others have carried for a similar route on blogs or by asking them.

879. With your own list, start from the body layer and work out. This means underwear first and you can carry spares for each day (hygienic and actually quite pleasant) or go for a merino option that is going to be functional for a few days.

Qasr al-Abd is a spectacular Hellenistic ruin in Jordan, so we ran past it for a picture. © *James Vincent*

This trail, in the Dana Biosphere in Jordan, was the first proper trail we'd seen in days so we just had to run a little bit more at the end of the day. © *James Vincent*

880. The other skin contact layer that's very important is your socks. Merino is great again for multiple days, plus it keeps its warmth when wet.

881. For women, a spare sports bra or crop top can be useful. Sweat and the salt that comes with it can really chafe, so it's better to have a spare to swap out and wash if really needed, as it will be soaking up that first layer of moisture.

882. Then start thinking about base layers. When travelling for multiple days, versatility is key and if a piece of kit can do more than one task, then great. For this reason, I usually go for a T-shirt base layer and separate arm warmers. It gives you more versatility than a long-sleeved top that can be too hot during the day.

883. Carrying a spare long-sleeved base layer might be your evening wear and an emergency layer combined. The same could be said for a pair of running tights if you need them for backup in the high mountains or just in the early morning chill.

884. Next come windproof and waterproof layers. Plan for the worst weather you can experience, rather than scrimping with lightweight kit, especially if you're in the mountains. Add in days of fatigue, low energy and tiredness, and you could find that a storm, which you'd brush off on a normal day outing, can become an epic survival battle.

885. Even if you don't think you need a windproof, pack one anyway. They're so lightweight and handy and it could be someone else who needs it.

886. When choosing shoes for an adventure, comfort is the main factor. You'll often have to make compromises if you're crossing different kinds of terrain and only able to take one pair, so take that into account. For Kom-Emine I needed something I could trust on road and rock, with everything in between, but there wasn't any rain expected so my choice was a road shoe that I trusted on dry trails too, the (now discontinued) New Balance Zante. Any more grip than that and I would have struggled on the hard-packed trails and road section.

887. A shoe that slows you down a little on more technical sections but allows you to enjoy the hard-packed miles is better than a shoe that lets you bomb it down the trails, but leaves you in discomfort for the majority of the trip. It's all very specific to your adventure, so do your research and figure out what is best for you.

888. A down jacket is your bezzy mate unless it's raining. Lightweight and packable, they're great to keep you warm at night and in colder conditions. If it's raining, down loses its warming ability very easily, so look at synthetic alternatives like PrimaLoft. This goes for any adventuring in Scotland when it can rain on any one (or possibly all) of the 365 days of the year.

889. Hats, a Buff® and gloves are a must. If you're up high during the day or staying high at night, then it will be colder than you expect.

890. A pair of plastic surgical gloves takes up no space and could be really useful *in extremis*. The same goes for a pair of women's tights. Under a pair of waterproof trousers, that extra layer can make a huge difference to warmth.

891. Same again for a space blanket. They're tiny and if someone busts an ankle (or just didn't pack any warm clothes) then you can wrap them in one and put their jacket over the top. They'll cook nicely.

892. Always cram in some extra rations of food at the bottom of your pack. Something you're not going to access unless you really need it. This could be some energy gels or an energy-packed flapjack, but if you get caught out and need it then it's worth all the hassle to get it out.

893. A favourite treat – dark chocolate, Haribo or some pork scratchings – can do wonders for morale if you're feeling low. It works for teammates too. If you know them well then secretly pack one of their preferences and produce it when they hit the wall for the third time that day.

894. A phone with a good camera is another item that ticks two boxes, but why stop there? You can use apps like Komoot to download your GPS route so you'll have a useful backup navigation device and even a torch for when someone's head torch goes. That's a last resort though.

895. With that in mind, an additional power pack isn't just emergency power for your devices, but a way to ensure your phone really is a backup for emergencies. Save your battery by turning off apps that download in the background and even consider airplane mode — you really don't need to send that nineteenth tweet.

896. If you are planning on night travel then pack a good main head torch and an adequate backup too. If you're only travelling in the day, you still need a decent option for early starts, getting lost and having to keep going after sunset, getting into a communal hostel late or just a surprise tunnel.

897. Whatever navigation device you go for, even if the trail is well marked, it's worth having a paper map and compass. If all your devices die in an EMP attack (or more likely they're out of juice) then the old-fashioned way will keep you safe.

898. If travelling solo then a small book could be really nice for the evenings. Chances are there might be other travellers to chat to, books in a refuge or just a beautiful sunset to savour instead though.

BIVVYING AND CAMPING (899–911)

899. If you want to wild camp or bivvy on the trail then great! It's a whole extra adventure and you'll need a bit more kit, but your scope for exploring increases tenfold. First things first; if you're a newbie, practise in your garden or a local campsite first.

900. Weight is important, but so is packability. If there is more than one of you then splitting the tent into its component parts and each carrying some will share the load. The same goes for any communal kit.

901. Lightweight tents are great, but can be an expensive option when a good bivvy will do the job. If you're not getting rained on, or can find good shelter, a bivvy can provide adequate sleeping requirements and you can do everything else outside.

902. Lightweight sleeping bags are another area where it's sensible to consider weight and packability. Super-lightweight can also mean not very warm, so find something that suits your requirements.

903. A silk liner can really increase the warmth of a sleeping bag without adding too much weight or bulk to your kit. So can sleeping in all your clothes or camping in a barn. Or a four-star hotel if it all goes Pete Tong.

Running will introduce you to brilliant people who share the same spirit of adventure. © *James Vincent*

904. It might seem unnecessary to include a floor mat, but you can lose an awful lot of heat to the ground, so it's worth the additional weight if you want a good night's sleep. You can even just make something yourself from bubble wrap or half a yoga mat that will make a difference.

905. When it comes to sleep quality, think about how long you'll be out on your trip too. One rubbish night of sleep on a two-day adventure won't change much, but if it's multiple nights then you'll regret not getting high-quality shut-eye.

906. A combination can work too – one night out wild camping, the next in a hotel or refuge. It still halves the accommodation costs (once you've deducted the cost of your fancy sleeping bag and tiny tent) and you can get away with a lighter camping or bivvy kit as you know the next night will be cosier.

907. If you're packing a stove to cook dinner and make coffee in the morning, then check you have enough gas before travelling. If flying to your adventure you might need to pick up gas upon arrival, so check out what will be available as you might need to take a certain stove.

908. A team of three should carry an extra stove, just for ease of heating water for everyone and making morning coffee, but also if your stove breaks.

909. If you're in the Alps and you can get your morning coffee at the mountain huts, then it's worth saving a bit of weight by not taking a stove. Have a cold breakfast, get moving early and then treat yourself to a wee break at the first cafe or bakery.

910. Pack a small repair kit with a needle and thread, duct tape, safety pins and some extra bits and bobs. You'll be surprised what you can fix in the field.

911. When sharing out kit to carry, take into account the ability and the size of the individual too. Don't be a hero if you're half the weight of one of your teammates and you're both carrying the same weight. It's a bigger percentage of your bodyweight so the impact is greater, but equally if you're fitter than everyone else, take a fair share. There's no point in lording it up from the top of each climb with a smug look if you could be helping the team.

Always be aware that a photographer may be hiding in the bushes, so make sure you're looking your best when running next to beautiful mountain lakes. © *Tim Lloyd*

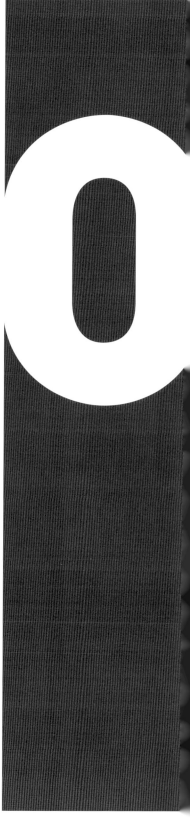

I've no idea how Heathcliff and Cathy found their way to The Grizzly in Devon.   © Pete Aylward, RunPhoto

009

STUFF (912–1001)

'If someone passes you it isn't automatically a challenge, despite what the wee chimp in your head says. Run your own run and don't start racing someone who might just be out for an easy, relaxing run after a hard day's work.'

STUFF (912-1001)

TRAIL AND TRACK ETIQUETTE
(912–932)

912. The road, track and the trail are all very different domains, but all have a set of unwritten rules for behaving around other runners and people. There aren't Strava police who'll pull you up, but a few rules are in place for good reason and will keep everyone happy.

913. When passing other runners and pedestrians it's good to let them know you're coming. If you're heavy footed like me then usually the slapping of your clown shoes on the ground can do the job, but next step might be a cough or other non-alarming noise.

914. Next step is a polite call out. It might just be a chirpy 'hello', '*bonjour*' or '*ciao*', but could also be instructive like 'coming past' or 'on your left'. There's a good chance when you say the latter that the person in front will still step directly into your path though.

915. Watch out for dog leads, especially extendable ones. They're invisible trip wires for unsuspecting runners trying to squeeze between dog and owner. Passing dogs can be sketchy, even if you are a fan of the hairy, four-legged wonders. They can be protective of owners, especially with children around. Yes, they should be on a lead if they like biting runners, but it's always good to let the owner know you're coming, slowing down a little and, if they do come for you, stop. Even if you're on an effort, it's better to interrupt it than get bitten.

916. If you're a dog owner, saying 'he's never bitten anyone' or 'she's only playing' doesn't help. A runner doesn't want to be the first bitten, nor do they always want to play.

917. If you're running past horse riders, take a similar approach. Slow down, to a walk if necessary, and make eye contact with and smile at the riders. Again, it might be a bit irritating if you're mid effort, but a spooked horse can throw their rider off or kick you in the face. If we all respect each other while enjoying the outdoors then the world will be a nicer place.

918. Depending on the environment, it's better to give way to the speedier mode of transport. Walker stands aside for runner; runner moves over for cyclist. It just means the pass happens quicker. If you're running uphill and a cyclist is bombing down on a lovely bit of single-track, then it'll only take you a second to stand to the side. Be kind to cyclists going uphill, as restarting on a hill is a pain. Remember too it only takes a few extra seconds to wait for someone who looks a bit unsure, or has kids with them or a nervous-looking hound. Even if you have the right of way and are mid interval, being a nice person is never a bad thing.

919. That said, see yourself as an ambassador for your sport regardless. It only takes a couple of extra seconds to let a group pass and you can give them a big smile at the same time. This makes everyone's day better and means that they'll be nicer to the next runner too.

920. Try not to do big puddle jumps when you're next to other people, unless they're your friends.

921. If you get to the point where you're doing big snot rockets (holding one side of your nose and blasting gunk out the other) then remember that's not acceptable while running through urban environments, particularly around others.

922. If you catch another runner up, don't just sit behind them. This goes especially for male runners behind female runners; it's creepy.

Top tip to improve your descending: marry a former British and English fell running champion. It's helped me bundles. © *Robbie Britton*

923. If someone passes you, it isn't automatically a challenge, despite what the wee chimp in your head says. Run your own run and don't start racing someone who might just be out for an easy, relaxing run after a hard day's work.

924. Saying hello and smiling at other runners is great and it can help spread some joy throughout the running community, but that other runner doesn't owe you a smile back. They might have had a rubbish day, be running their last interval or just not feel comfortable engaging with others on a dark road or trail. Like presents, don't give running smiles just to get them back.

925. The track has a whole different set of rules, some written down, others not. Figuring them out, just from observing what others are doing, helps everything along. If you take your kids or friends who are new to the track for a workout, then give them a quick run-down of the normal rules.

926. Lane one (the inside lane) is for running hard. I'm using 'hard' instead of 'fast' here, because if you're doing 400-metre intervals and you're not that fast then you still deserve to use lane one.

927. If you're doing a warm-up then your best bet is to use the outside lanes or find a loop nearby. If the track is empty then you can do what you like, but if others are working out and you're pootling along to start your run then it's better to give them some space.

928. Look both ways before you cross the track just as you would when crossing a road. People will most likely always come from the same direction but always check if you're crossing lanes.

929. If you are doing an easy lap between intervals then you don't need to hit lane eight, but you could use lane two or three. If you only have one lap for recovery, it'll give you an extra seven metres to chill per lane.

930. Running with headphones is frowned upon by some on the track, but if you do like to use them then be aware of those around you.

931. If someone is in your way then shout 'track' and try to smile (effort dependent of course). It doesn't need to sound aggressive, although if it keeps happening then it might inevitably start to.

932. If you prefer a quieter workout, try to find out when the track is used by clubs or groups. On the other hand, if there is a group on the track then you might be able to join in, if it's the right kind of session for you.

RUNNING WITH YOUR DOG
(933-944)

933. Running with our four-legged friends can be absolutely wonderful. If we all approached life with the same joy, trust and blind love that dogs do then the world would be a better place, although there would be more arse sniffing.

934. You can either get a new puppy or provide a home for a rescue dog, both have their pros and cons in terms of finding your new training partner though.

935. A new puppy, whatever the breed, can't be guaranteed to grow up to be a runner; whereas with a rescue dog you can find out a little about their energy and activity levels before adoption.

Petra the super hound joined us for the second half of the Jordan Trail and then we found her a new family at the beach. © *James Vincent*

936. A new puppy also needs time to grow, so in the first 12 or 18 months you shouldn't go running with your dog. They'll run about and charge all over the place off the lead, but they're still growing so that needs to be respected.

937. A rescue dog can certainly be harder work, but there are so many around and they need your love. You can also pick a good runner from the get-go, as the staff at the rescue centre will know which dogs have the most energy.

938. Speak to other runners with dogs before making any decisions as there are plenty of great breeds for running. We have German shorthaired pointers – they're ace on the trail and have a lovely nature too.

939. Any dog is likely to cover a lot more ground than you when they're off the lead. For every kilometre you run they'll likely double it by going back and forth, through bushes, chasing scents and exploring. When a dog runs off the lead they cover more ground, but it's at their own pace and style. It'll be more like an interval run than the steady effort we put out. They're built to run fast and recover fast.

940. If you have a dog on the lead then keep in mind they may need to stop and recover, lay some super-important scents or just be overheating or getting tired because they haven't had a break. Even the most endurance-focused hounds love an interval.

941. If you're going further afield then take some food and water for your dog if you need to. Yes, they will happily drink from the grungiest of puddles and eat a whole load of rubbish they find on the trail, but I'm not sure fox poo is that nutritious and you can't count on puddles on hot days.

942. Dogs have a less effective thermo-regulation system than we do. They need to pant and can also lose heat through their paws, so if they're too hot then keep this in mind. They can't sweat on the go like we do – imagine trying to stay cool just by hanging your tongue out of your mouth.

943. At the height of summer, check the ground temperature before you run as if it's too hot for your hand then it could damage your dog's paws.

944. Learn from your dog, they're smarter than you might imagine. Hard run? An afternoon sleeping on the sofa. Too hot? Hide in the shade for a bit. Foraging on the trail? Actually they set a pretty bad example there.

STUFF (912–1001)

TOILETS ON THE RUN (945–954)

945. This is an area where we really shouldn't copy the example of our four-legged friends, but sometimes nature just calls.

946. Getting used to this part of running can be difficult for some runners, but you can improve the situation with a few tweaks and be better prepared for disaster too.

947. Pack yourself a kit for if you're caught short. All it needs to be is a bit of toilet roll and some Imodium® if you're out on a longer run and think you'll need it, all packed ready in a small plastic bag to take with you. If you're particularly prone to a bad stomach, just having a couple of kits ready to grab as you're leaving the house can be a real help.

948. Suitable little plastic bags can be found on the internet in either the stationery or the drug paraphernalia section. They can have a whole load of uses, such as sorting out food portions for a race, keeping your iPod dry or, as above, packing a little bit of toilet roll that doesn't then get soaked by your sweat.

949. If you are caught short then the first option should always be a proper toilet. In urban environments you might be lucky and find a public toilet; other good options are pubs and betting shops (these all have to have a toilet). Ask nicely and people are generally happy to let you use the loo.

950. The next option is getting in the bushes. It's not great form to poo in bushes in the city, but sometimes you just can't help it. Get as far off the track or trail as you can and face towards the trail, so you don't moon anyone who happens to walk past.

951. If you've been smart and packed your toilet paper in a little plastic bag then it's good to carry a spare bag so you can pack up your loo roll and drop it in the nearest bin. No need to litter if you can help it.

952. If you're on a bigger adventure and don't want to carry out a load of used toilet roll with you, then carrying a lighter to burn the paper is another option. If you were in Antarctica, you'd have to carry out all your waste, including the poo.

953. For number ones it's obviously easier for the chaps than the ladies, but we should still be considerate of where we are. Don't just pee on someone's garden wall at the start of every run, you feral beast.

954. When training for the Tor des Géants, a 330-kilometre mountain race in Italy, I suggested to my wife that she could practise peeing close to the trail. It's an event that goes to some really wild places; the blokes just stepped to the side of the trail to have a wee, whereas I found that Nats and other female runners were adding on loads of extra kilometres by climbing to somewhere hidden. These days, I turn around mid conversation on a trail run and she's weeing next to me at the side of the trail and I couldn't be prouder.

MUSIC (955–964)

955. Music makes you run faster. Well, good music does. Playing too much Celine Dion might make you cry when you run.

956. If you are doing a hard session or some intervals, then music has been proven to make you push a bit harder. It's either just getting into a good rhythm or disassociating with the pain at hand, but it works.

957. If your intervals are longer than one song (or you're listening to really short songs) then don't look at your watch until the end of the song. Working too hard for that? Hold out until the chorus, then try to sing it out loud between breaths.

958. Started too hard on your progression runs? Plan a playlist with some Bob Marley to start, build it up a little in the middle with some of The Strokes and then hit the drum and bass for the final push. Obviously you can insert your own tastes into the appropriate section of the run.

959. If you're one of the lucky people whose ears are perfect for any head-phones then I'm very jealous. I've always needed ones that hook around the back of my ears and they have a limited time span for me due to high levels of sweat. I might just be extra sweaty (very likely), but when given the choice between expensive and cheaper headphones I've stopped spending too much as I know they'll break eventually.

960. It's worth running with just one ear in to keep a good awareness of traffic and other people around you. That's another plus point of cheap headphones – you can still hear a lot of the noise around you.

961. If you're racing, make sure that headphone use is within the rules. When races go on to open roads or cross over roads, it can be a disqualifying offence to wear headphones. Some race rules allow for headphones that work through bone-conduction instead.

962. If racing in an ultra, use your music wisely. It can be best not to have it pumping from the start and overdo things, but that also goes for the latter stages of a race as well. Too often I have seen runners chuck music on at the halfway point and then hit the wall a few kilometres down the trail. You're likely to be on a bit of a knife-edge with your energy levels, and if music changes your perception of effort, it can knock that fine balance out of kilter.

963. For long races it can also be nice to get friends and family to suggest songs or even create a playlist for you. The positive memories and smiles this brings can be an added boost. If you're feeling super fancy then get friends to record positive or funny messages that you can play between songs as well.

964. For longer races and training there are loads of great podcasts and audio-books you can enjoy. Downloading some funny podcasts will certainly make the easy kilometres go by, but beware of the impact of laughing maniacally when running on your own. The neighbours may think that you've finally lost it. Equally, there are some great podcasts out there and it can really feel like you're using your time well if you're learning something new when out running too. Whether it's history, training philosophy or learning a new language, it can provide a double whammy for productivity so you can be extra smug about your run.

We can't tell you what TSHFG stands for on the T-shirt as it's a bit rude. We did see a Chinook while taking the photo though, which was cool.   © *John Coefield*

STUFF (912-1001)

SAFETY FIRST (965-976)

965. It's a driver's job to be focused on the road, and trying to avoid hitting runners, cyclists, pedestrians (and other vehicles), not playing on their phone. I certainly don't want these tips to come across as blaming road accidents on the victims, but there are a few things we can do to make sure our untimely death from Albert in his Fiat Panda is less likely.

966. Firstly, assume drivers haven't seen you unless you can see the whites of their eyes and they're smiling at you, while nodding that you should cross first. Even then, be wary. Yes, you might be smashing that PB segment, but it's not worth being bounced off a car bonnet.

967. Remember that in some countries it's actually frowned upon to use your indicator and drivers actually communicate through telepathy. Or guesswork. It's clearly one or the other. In other words, if running somewhere new, especially overseas, bear in mind that the accepted customs can be different.

968. The same goes for driveways. Assume drivers have not seen you running along the pavement as they are usually looking for pedestrians and cars. Runners, especially those at high velocity, can come as a shock.

969. During the day, it's up to you if you want to wear bright clothes. If you want to make yourself more visible, then high-vis yellow-green is apparently in fashion. We wore high-vis vests for the LEJOG record with Dan Lawson and no one was hit by a car. Dan ran mostly topless though and he wasn't hit either.

970. If you're running at night then reflective kit is best. Let those massive headlights do most of the work. Be safe, be seen. Wearing some reflective kit is going to let drivers and cyclists wonder what is in front of them a couple of seconds sooner and hopefully stop them ploughing into you.

971. Some higher-end head torches come with a flashing red light on the back, but there are also a few brands that make these separately too. These can weigh very little and really increase how visible you are at night.

972. Reflective bands on the bits of you that move, I'm talking arms and legs, are also effective. Apparently, the bio-mechanical movement triggers something in the brain of those who see it. You are now starting to look like an extra in a Daft Punk video, but your risk of sudden death has gone down too.

973. When running in poorly lit urban areas or remote places, try to be aware of your surroundings. You might want to run with your music pumping, but it's helpful to keep your senses alert, even if that means running with only one headphone in.

974. If running somewhere remote, then let a friend or family member know where you're going and when you expect to be back. Most of the time this isn't useful, but if something does happen then you have someone looking out for you and, if you're more remote, then a rescue team can be helped by these simple details.

975. Safety isn't just avoiding injury or impact with a car, but also feeling safe yourself. It might be from avoiding areas with poor street lighting, running with friends at night or always having a phone with you for emergencies.

STUFF (912-1001)

976. As a fast, male runner with a big facial scar, I sometimes struggle to relate to other runners feeling unsafe. Having said that, I have been threatened and attacked when running in dodgy areas, but I still have that confidence that I can outrun most trouble. Keep in mind that everyone has different levels of confidence and safety with their running; we should never dismiss someone's concerns about safety. Try to relate, empathise and help.

BLOGGING (977–993)

977. You've finished the toughest race of your life and want to tell people about it. Your options these days are blogging, vlogging or podcasting.

978. With any of these options, think about two things: can I make this funny or can I make this useful? Otherwise, the only use is a cathartic release for yourself and that might as well be a 'dear diary … ' moment.

979. I'll start with vlogging, as I know the least about this. Many people make this look easy and seamless on YouTube, but actually a lot of hard work and know-how goes into it. Start your own vlogging adventures by investigating some of the more successful examples online. Don't limit yourself to running ones either. Really, please don't.

980. Good cameras are important, but good sound is vital. People will watch poor quality video with great sound but will turn off great video with poor sound. A tiny microphone with a wind cover costs very little and you can clip them to your collar.

981. This is even more vital with podcasting. If you sound like you're speaking from a cave in deepest Afghanistan then it's going to the difficult for people to enjoy your podcast, no matter how funny or informative it is.

982. When deciding to embark on your podcasting journey, ask yourself if it's adding anything to an already crowded space. By all means, do it for your own enjoyment, but if you want to get sponsorship or support, bring something new to the table.

983. With both vlogging and podcasts it's not just as simple as pressing record and then sending the raw file out on to the internet. The time and skill taken to do postproduction work on your efforts is vital and, if you can't be bothered to learn about that, consider paying someone to do it for you.

984. Blogging is something I do have experience of. For however many years now I've been churning out articles and advice pieces, and editing other people's work too. Here are some basic rules to help you make something interesting that people might enjoy reading.

985. If you can't say it in 1,000 words then shorten it. The internet generation spends a few seconds scanning loads of different articles, rather than sitting down in an armchair next to a fire to enjoy a story. If you want to reach more than your immediate family, then set yourself a limit; 800 to 1,000 words are usually plenty if you're succinct. Be brutal as your own editor.

986. Start with a hook. Something interesting enough to attract the reader and make them want to continue reading. Even the most dedicated friend will start to scan the words pretty quickly if it's not interesting, so get something worth reading into the first paragraph.

987. Try to make your writing useful. Just writing about your own experience might be helpful to someone trying to do the same race or trying to learn about our sport, but if you make a concerted effort for this to happen, then your blog is adding something to the world at least.

Twenty-four-hour races always start fast, but none of the top finishers can be seen in the front row here. © *Robbie Britton*

STUFF (912-1001)

988. Don't just start at the beginning and travel all the way to the end, like many people do. Pluck out the usual information and funny stories and combine them in a way that takes the reader along the way with you. If everything happened in the second half of the race, don't spend half your blog getting there. Even a simple 'it was all going so smoothly until kilometre 70 … ' could suffice in getting you to the good stuff.

989. Take your time with a good title. It's likely that's all most people will ever see, especially if the title is rubbish.

990. Please use humour. Even if it is a deeply emotional, reflective piece, a bit of smiling will help people enjoy your writing. A point is more likely to sink in if it makes someone feel something and humour is a good tool for this.

991. Be honest. Remember that most of your audience will either be experienced at running or will become so in the future. You don't need to make what you're doing sound epic if it actually is, because that comes through. Don't exhaust your superlatives too early in the piece either.

992. Stick to the word count. Yes, some people will read it if you write 5,000 words, but are they really 5,000 useful words? Surely you can cut out some of the superfluous garbage. It's not like you've got a commission to write *1001 Running Tips* and have to drag the last 50 out of thin air because you've run out of ideas …

993. Enjoy your writing, vlogging or podcasting. You shouldn't find it a chore and if you do, that will come across. If you're not enjoying the process, then find a better use of your time. If you want sponsors, then most of the time just doing a paper round in the morning will bring in more cash (and there are extra cardio gains to be had), and if you're just after some attention, try kidnapping the Queen or something.

SOCIAL MEDIA (994-1001)

994. Don't waste too much time on social media. If you find you haven't got the time to get out of the door for a 30- to 45-minute run, delete all your social media apps and you'll have the time for an ultra every day.

995. When on social media, remember that this is the image and lifestyle someone has chosen for you to see. Seek out honesty and you'll have a much more useful and enjoyable time. A constant feed of people running faster than you, smiling more and having a better sex life does not make happy viewing and is rarely the whole truth.

996. If you want to chart your own journey, remember that, like your training, consistency is the most important thing for getting more followers. Unlike training, it doesn't matter if it's just lies and poor-quality nonsense, constant noise works on social media. In training it pays to be smart, but on social media, not so much.

997. Look for good people to follow, from runners and coaches who inspire you to your favourite scientists and researchers. On Instagram, watch out for those who post 15 times a day, as that's all you'll see.

998. Look for people's bias and conflicts of interest. If you're getting bombarded by 17 different tweets about the same pair of socks being brilliant, it's more than likely a targeted and scheduled media push for the brand, rather than simultaneous sock love from your favourite runners.

999. If you want to do well on Instagram then take the time to get nice pictures, maybe from a fancy phone or GoPro, learn from people who know more than you and enjoy experimenting with different types of shot. If you can't be bothered with that, then just pay a professional photographer to follow you around and take awesome pictures all the time.

If you look like this after your warm-up then maybe start a little easier. © *Tim Lloyd*

1000. Don't underestimate the time and effort some of the social media superstars put into their accounts. It's all made to look seamless and easy, but proper 'Instagrammers' are probably spending more time on their pictures than their actual running. If you're happy seeing your PBs lower in line with your followers rising, then crack on.

1001. Last tip: don't listen to me about social media. I'm an old man now and much prefer writing things than taking pictures, videos or creating memes. If you enjoy social media, that's great – go and inspire a whole bunch of other runners to love the sport like you do and make the world a better place. I'll be sitting in the corner, reading an old-fashioned proper book and grumbling about the 'youth of today'.

Cobbles in running are a lot friendlier than in cycling, but they still can get a bit slippery when wet. © *Tim Lloyd*

When wearing sunglasses, remember to put them over your eyes, instead of on your head, when it's sunny. © *Robbie Britton*

010

READING LIST

'This book may feel like it has all the tips, but it's just a starting point. If you want to learn more, then here are some great places to start.'

READING LIST

A selection of books, websites and people I've found useful in my own never-ending search for best practice.

Endurance Performance in Sport edited by Carla Meijen
Routledge, 2019.
ISBN: 9781138053212
Research into human psychology and interventions within endurance sports from some of the best in the field.

Endure by Alex Hutchinson
HarperCollins, 2019.
ISBN: 9780008308186
Any article by Alex Hutchinson is worth a read and his book is an enjoyable journey through his own investigations into what makes us endure.

Fast Fuel: Food for Running Success by Renee McGregor
Nourish, 2016.
ISBN: 9781848993099
It's important to learn about your own nutrition and Renee provides an evidence-based but understandable insight into fuelling our training and racing.

Feed Zone Portables by Biju Thomas and Allen Lim
VeloPress, 2013.
ISBN: 9781937715007
If you're not a fan of the normal sports drinks and products then this is a good place for recipes to make your own.

Mindset by Carol Dweck
Robinson, 2017.
ISBN: 9782133487514
It's all well and good knowing what training and racing you need to do, but making sure you have the right mindset to learn from your experiences and grow is also essential.

Training for Ultra Running by Andy Milroy
JMD Media, 2013.
ISBN: 9781780913247
A collection of articles and chapters from some of the greatest ultra-runners of the past. It's full of great (and slightly less great) ideas that led to the successes of athletes like Don Ritchie, Yiannis Kouros and Eleanor Robinson.

Broken by Ally Beaven
Vertebrate Publishing, 2020.
ISBN: 9781839810404
A wonderful, inspiring insight into a whole host of record-breaking runs in the summer of 2020. Ally's a nice chap too, which shines through.

For the most part, the books that have taught me the most are ones like John Porter's *One Day as a Tiger* or Joe Tasker's *Savage Arena*. If you want to really learn about endurance and perseverance, then the mountaineers take the biscuit.

There are plenty of great websites for running information, but make sure you can tell the difference between good advice and advertisements (although they can be both). *Runner's World*, *Athletics Weekly*, *Fast Running* and the US *LetsRun.com* are some of my favourites. Google Scholar is your best bet if you want some actual advice though.